A Penny for the Ploughboys

Songs, Tunes & Choruses
and
Settings to Traditional songs
Reminiscences on a lifetime's folk experience
and the nature of folk tradition
by
Colin Cater

Edited & Illustrated by Karen Cater

Design by Karen Cater

Hedingham Fair

www.hedinghamfair.co.uk

Published in Great Britain
by Hedingham Fair 2009

Copyright © Colin Cater 2009
Illustrations © Karen Cater

ISBN: 978-0-9556475-1-2

Printed in Great Britain by
Healeys Printers
Ipswich

www.Hedinghamfair.co.uk

To

Everyone with whom I have ever shared a pint or a
song or an idea - you are all here

Singers, musicians and Morris Dancers everywhere
you will never grow old!

THANKS

Thanks to Karen for a million things:
for listening for a seemingly interminable time while ideas crystallized;
for instantaneous thoughts that relieved writing blocks;
for singing and playing on many of the songs;
for her vision and typesetting, turning songs and ideas into a book

Thanks to Anahata and Mary:
for liberal quantities of food, beer and good company;
for use of Treewind Studios and playing in the studio recordings;
for organising and supervising the recordings and mastering;
for transcribing the music

Thanks to Derek Connell for use of the Three Horseshoes, Duton Hill

Thanks to Dave Holland for some thoughtful fiddling

Thanks to Everyone who came and sang the choruses

CONTENTS

Introduction

This book and CD are designed to provide a showcase for songs and tunes written by Colin Cater, most of them in recent years.

"When I was younger my folk experience was very rich – six nights a week pretty often. How my family ever stood it, I'll never know!! One of the consequences was that I set my face against certain things, simply because there wasn't enough room in my life - being a Morris Dancer was one. I also determined that folk music would be my hobby, untainted with the quasi-academic gobbledegook that my professional life brought. I would enjoy my hobby intuitively, for the joy of being. In particular, I would avoid learning to read music, not to be chained by the printed page, but concentrate on being able to hear music accurately and play it back straight away if possible. Only in later years did I come to think I had hobbled myself – and that being able to poodle around in 'Bronson' would be every bit as much fun as romping through 'Child'. So I was never much of a researcher, which perhaps is a bit of a handicap for anyone aspiring to a reputation as a folk performer, which I always

Colin at home 2009

hankered after just a bit. As I got older, I cared less and less what the tunes were anyway. Part of me groaned at hearing the same old songs in the same old versions again and again . . . and again. Wouldn't it be nice if some of them came out in a slightly different form? Well, to cut a long story short . . .

I didn't see myself as a natural song or tune writer, having rubbed shoulders with friends who could do this standing on their heads, or so it seemed. It's important to have something to write about, although sometimes having a good catch phrase can be very useful. Several themes run through this small collection – principally the ideas of the passage of the seasons. You can't be a Morris Dance musician for long without celebrating on May morning or deciding to do a Mummers Play or getting involved in any number of activities at the turn of the year that have precious little to do with Christmas. After Hedingham Fair started in 1997, it became a way of life. It's also impossible to be involved with ceremonial without giving some thought to ritual, religion and belief. I had cast off the shackles of Christianity as a young man and have never since been able to view it as more than one

2

mythology among many, though the notion of 'higher authority' or the need to develop spiritually perhaps over more than one lifetime have always seemed very significant. I'm also convinced that English traditions have more that one antecedent belief system and I have been keen that the songs should reflect this

I'd like to think I've had an interesting folk life: singing has always been central, in a church choir as a boy treble, then in folk music once I'd grasped that its lyrics were far more developed and sensible than anything offered by 1950s and 60s pop. Learning that many of the American songs in the 1960s charts had British / European origins and had undergone a cultural journey to their then current state, and could go further in the hands of talented songwriters was very formative. As I increasingly delved into British music, it became awkward to reconcile this with the grandeur of many of the country singers still available to be listened to 'up close and personal'. Alternative approaches based on folk music and 'traditional music' run right through the writing: when I was young it was very apparent that the fledgling folk movement was teetering on a knife edge between conflicting ideologies, and that after the passing of Bert Lloyd and Ewan MacColl, it was likely

At Treewind Studios 2009

that the backwards looking view would prevail. What couldn't be foreseen in the middle of the 1960s was the extent to which singing would decline in favour of instrumental music and dance, as the guitar became superseded by the melodeon.

Although I took up the melodeon eagerly, I lamented the seemingly gradual sidelining of lyric creativity in favour of standardised repertoire; the reaction against writing about contemporary events in favour of the rural idyll of a century or more ago; the sense that it was somehow not quite acceptable as a singer to explore the potentiality of contemporary and cheap instrumental technology. Too many people for my comfort thought they understood what tradition was / is, when in my view they didn't, or at least that their understandings were different from mine. It took a long time to develop a carefully argued self-view of folk tradition, as set out in these pages. In particular, the question "How had the folk traditions of England developed?" had to be addressed, followed by questions about what sort of environment we live in now and whether explanations as to how traditions developed in the past still applied, or whether an alternative model is needed to understand folk tradition now. Unfortunately many of the social conditions which gave rise to these traditions no longer exist in (most of) Britain, and with social changes have come changes in the ways in which songs and other folk activities are transmitted between people. In the main text I put forward what I call a 'variant transmission' model that might explain development of the ballad and song repertoire recovered by the great folk collections of early C20 (and afterwards). Unfortunately this simply does not explain how songs, tunes and dances have been transmitted between people throughout C20 / C21. Yet folk transmission between people, without the intervention of mass media, still takes place. A revised model through which to understand folk tradition is thus necessary – more inclusive than some previous models and definitely incorporating contemporary creativity, as always happened until folklorists invented 'oral tradition'. The more I looked at this issue, the more I was drawn to the approach put forward in William Chappell's Popular Music of the Olden Time.

In this book, and on the CD is a small collection of songs, tunes and settings for existing traditional songs I've developed, mainly in the last few years. Supporting the project is quite a lot of writing – more than I'd intended when it started.

Recording at The Three Horseshoes, Duton Hill, near Thaxted, Essex, *l to r - Adrian Hilton, Joe Hobbs, Mike & Niki Acott, Paul O'Kelly, Paul McCann, Colin*

4

The Three Horseshoes where 'Penny for the Ploughboys' live tracks were recorded, here shown during 'PensionFest' - Thaxted Morris Men and Witchmen dance for Colin's 65th birthday party

Although I have quoted many of the sources I've used, the book is intended for anyone to read, and for this reason is not referenced to a full academic standard. Pete Coe has been kind enough to take the title song 'Penny for the Ploughboys' out to a wider audience but most of the other new songs are not well known. They are a by-product of a lifetime of love for England's vernacular traditions, with which I am involved daily as part of Hedingham Fair with Karen. We didn't set out to write songs to complement designs, or yet the other way round – it just seemed like a good thing to do. Nearly all the songs are written in a mixture of old fashioned styles. Little bits of the thinking are Pagan, but that has been as much to take English music to a Pagan world hung up on any cultural bus that passes, as to Paganise folk traditions. One song – High Plains of Afghanistan, a recasting of Lowlands of Holland – is overtly political. Over the years I have written other political songs, but they tend to have a short shelf life and I don't remember most of them a few months later.

Lots of the songs have pretty good (so I'm told) choruses, so it seemed a natural thing to record them in a live session with a pub room stuffed full of old friends. What a cracking night it was too! I'd like to thank Derek Connell, the landlord of the Three Horseshoes, Duton Hill, Essex for letting us use his room. Let's hope he never has to have Stansted Airport as his back garden. I'd also like to thank all fifty five people who came, raised the rafters and put up with having to do it again 'until we got it right'. Both the live session and the studio bashes at 'Treewind Studios' were supervised by Anahata and Mary Humphreys, to whom many thanks for making and mixing the recordings; for putting up with me when I wanted to do it again because I was under rehearsed; for their own splendid musical contributions; for transcribing the music, also for inviting Dave Holland, whose superb fiddle playing can be heard on several tracks, to be part of the project. But most of all I'd like to thank Karen, whose care and whose artistic talents have been my inspiration for over a decade and a half, whose wonderful illustrations illuminate the book, and whose inventive percussion and ever critical eye and ear have contributed enormously to every stage of the development of the book and CD.

Recollections - a Lifetime in Folk Music

Starting Out – the Singing Years

I was born in 1943 as a wartime evacuee into a family whose lifestyle involved regular work relocations – a pattern of peripatetic life which would continue until I landed in Essex in 1970. I lived in turn in Stourbridge, Bristol, Penarth, Harrogate, Reading, London, Nottingham and Clay Cross, Derbyshire, more than that my knowledge of England and the English was strengthened immeasurably by four years working as a semi pro folkie (1966 – 70) and all the Midlanders, Geordies, Scots, East Anglians, Cornishmen, Irishmen and others with whom I rubbed shoulders and shared pints in smoke filled rooms and endlessly put the world to rights with. The question "Where do you come from" was never an easy one.

Edward Colin
Cater
born 19-9-1943

Early experiences of folk song came at school in Penarth. I groaned with the apples leaning down low in Linden Lea and blew with the Winter Wind – thank goodness for Sospan Fach and a bit of hwyl boyo! On reflection I suppose these were 'National' songs rather than folksongs. Cecil Sharp obviously never got through the Severn Tunnel (bridge not yet built) and in any case once Lonnie Donegan and then the Kingston Trio / Peter Paul and Mary / Highwaymen / Dylan came along all folk music was American, an illusion which took time and relocation to Yorkshire to unlearn.

Before I left South Wales in 1958, I'd developed the habit of going over to Cardiff after school in search of the latest records. One Department Store on St Mary Street (David Morgan I think) had installed listening booths where you could play the latest American chart singles, before they became well known over here. Endless hours of delight and they didn't seem to mind if you never bought anything. British Rock'n'Roll was, by common consent, crap – OK at frantic but never, never sexy – a situation remedied eventually by the Beatles, Stones and all that came after. In the meantime, the record booths were a godsend for the aspiring musical snob. In Harrogate, things weren't so easy. You had to ask the assistant in the record shop to play the single you wanted and their tolerance soon wore thin if you didn't buy. But a group of us used to congregate after school to walk down into town earnestly discussing which were the more progressive of the new releases. One night Robin (1), who went to the posh school up the road, asked if we had heard of Lester Flatt and Earl Scruggs – blank faces all round. Apparently Scruggs was a Billy Whizz banjo player, and we were dragged down to Ron's Record Store in the underground market – but all the Scruggs records had been sold, probably to Robin anyway.

About the same time a folk club was starting up in Harrogate, meeting on Saturday nights, an offshoot of the local CND. This didn't exactly endear it to me – the issues (I'd rather be red than dead) had been endlessly debated at school and the mutual deterrence argument was persuasive – surely we were better off with the bomb than without it. In any case, having been educated liberally by my family and through the grammar school system, I had a clear sense of my own individuality. All this collectivism and 'unity is strength' stuff was for someone else. Eventually I was to learn who, but for the time being, Saturday nights were for the coffee bar, ice ink, dance hall, pub and anywhere else where there were girls on the look out for a good time. From time to time I'd run into Robin who by that time was playing the banjo pretty well and had a band playing bluegrass music, the Crimple Mountain Boys (2). (Crimple Beck ran through the local ICI works in Harrogate and over several miles of predominately flat landscape nearby). Eventually Robin persuaded me to come to the club held in a pub called The Empress in a darkened upstairs room, where for a modest consideration paid to a blousy woman outside the door of the club room, you could sit in your duffle coat, shiver on an upturned beer crate and listen to the collected folk talent of Harrogate. The favourite song was Captain Kidd, a grisly nautical murder ballad, but in which the bad guy eventually got his just desserts. 'Yellow Girls' got sung pretty regularly, 'Fourpence a Day' and the 'Celebrated Working Man'. But the Crimples ruled the roost and the penny that folk was English rather than American still didn't drop.

Looking back, I suppose the world must have found folk music before I did, though it doesn't seem like it when you're young. Several record shops in Harrogate had embryonic folk sections – the three Joan Baez albums released by Fontana, mainly consisting of Anglo-American ballads were soon forming the basis of many local singers' repertoires. In the local W. H. Smith, I bought James Reeves book 'Idiom of the People' about Cecil Sharp's collections and then Sharp's own polemic 'English Folksongs – Some Conclusions' and the club, which soon moved to the more plush surroundings of the West Park Hotel, was populated with an ever increasing number of idiosyncratic but strong personalities. There was the Dickensian Rennie (3), a young bloke called Dave (4) from Bradford with an enormous voice, Martin (5) who played Flamenco guitar rather expansively and Pash (6), a blues man from Leeds. I was drawn to Bert (7), an earnest chap, younger than he seemed, with face hidden in never ending hair overhanging a white Arran sweater. He was a supercilious sod, but with wide cultural horizons and experience and strong opinions about everything, but he was different – a bohemian, a beatnik (this was nearly a decade before hippies came on the scene) and he could play the guitar in a way that I don't think I've ever heard since, like a lute, very accurate and clipped, to accompany himself singing songs like the 'Seeds of Love' and 'Robin Hood and the Fifteen Foresters'. On occasion he'd invite me and my mate Dick to his house to drink mead and contemplate infinity – it was here I first heard the 'God thinks he's Ewan MacColl' joke. Who was Ewan MacColl anyway? Hadn't he had a chart hit with a cover version of 'Sixteen Tons'? It wouldn't be long before my horizons broadened.

One Saturday night Harrogate Folk Club booked its first guest singer, paying the princely sum of £25 for Josh MacRae, a Scots geezer who'd had a chart hit with a song called 'Messing about on the River'. Bert said it would have been a better use of the money if they'd let him wipe his arse with it, and suggested that we'd do much better to come over to the Union Tavern in Leeds the following Wednesday where Louis Killen was the guest singer. Leeds, Christ, man that's like going to Africa! but very gingerly we got on the train. Leeds Central station was a miserable place, always wet but we sidled stealthily out of it, crept under the bridges, past where the Grove Folk Club still stands and through the mean streets, now long knocked down, of Hunslet and Holbeck to the Tavern, also long gone. While not a Road to Damascus experience what followed was very formative. The resident group were pretty OK but Killen was a revelation – here was a voice, a singer, a style and a storyteller all rolled into one. It was difficult to maintain enough concentration to keep listening, although it was an art learned quickly. Come 10.30 when the pub shut and we had to run for the last train I must have been the last one out. Ron's record store had an EP of Louis called Northumbrian Minstrelsy that I quickly hoovered up. Leeds became a regular foray, to the Tavern, to the Memphis on Thursday and to Bob and Carole's (8) club on Sunday – pause to genuflect in front of memories of Tommy Gilfellon singing 'Oakee Strike Evictions' – breathtaking. By now the penny had dropped. Folk music was as much English as American, more than that it was about ordinary people all around us and things we could see and touch; coal, pits, mills, pubs, beer – it wasn't like pop music with its puerile rhyming, it was real.

Colin on stage in the Great Hall at Reading University
l to r: Marian Gray (Thameside Four); Bert Worth; Roger Watson (standing); Cyril Tawney (with Guitar); Colin; Dave Blagrove (behind Colin); Ian Truman.

In 1962, I'd gone to University at Reading and for a while folk music went on to the back burner in favour of jazz, R & B and the endless stream of wonderful young talent playing the Students Union dances on Saturdays and soon to illuminate the British Rock scene for decades. Folk was getting on the telly – the Tonight programme, The Hootenany show, quite a lot on Sunday evenings. More was

coming on the radio, Ewan MacColl's 'Song Carrier' programmes, 'As I Roved Out', the Radio Ballads, Bert Lloyd's wonderful documentary on the Elliott Family of Birtley, Co Durham. There was a good folk column in Melody Maker, including jottings about the London folk scene and a thorough gig list. I went up one evening to the Black Horse in Rathbone Place. There were some blokes playing guitars not particularly well I thought (Bert's prejudices had been influential) and then this Geordie with a shock of red hair and the most powerful voice I'd ever heard got up and sang 'Down you go, Jack'. I didn't take to Bob Davenport when I spoke to him afterwards, but what a voice!

In the months that followed several things happened. I was walking home to Earley one evening when who should be in front but Bert, from Harrogate, who said he was coming up to Reading in the autumn and would definitely get a folk club going. In due course Reading Ethnics was born – a time when to be ethnic was to glorify the culture of your own country, rather than to be part of someone else's minority – in the never to be forgotten surroundings of the Marquis of Granby, Cemetery Junction. It was a poky little room dominated by a pair of RAOB (the Buffaloes) horns at one end. Unless it was cold the windows had to be open so that the singers competed with the traffic noise and you could look out above the trolley bus wires and the serried ranks of Berkshire's departed. But it was heaven. Nearly all the singers were students struggling for repertoire. The one regular townie was Dave Blagrove, who seemed like an old boy even though he'd only just become a Dad, but who was special, having only just finished plying his trade as one of the last of the full time 'boaties' on the Grand Union Canal and who had a goodly stock of his own songs including 'Berkshire Tragedy' and 'Boatie, Boatie, shit in the cut', to which he would eventually add his own writing, songs like 'Single Bolinder', based on the Geordie mining song, 'Little Chance'. Once I'd got the singing bug, I learned almost anything that crossed my path and in a couple of years had a bulging song book. Most songs came from records, some from books with tunes gleaned from other singers, some just by hearing them sung live once. As long as songs were from somewhere in the British Isles they were OK – later worries surrounding pursuits like whaling and foxhunting hadn't yet emerged, although the idea that you should find and sing (even create) songs from your own locality was becoming more widely accepted. With West Country parents and having recently lived in Yorkshire and South Wales, I had difficulties with this. We were encouraged to sing unaccompanied – that's easy if you don't play anything. But if we wanted to entertain or to energise (urban) people who hadn't discovered 'folk' yet, surely a bit more than the solo voice would be needed. For the moment I formed a strong attachment to the industrial songs of the North and Midlands and quickly learned to imitate my hero, Louis.

At more or less the same time, a folk club started in Guildford, about twenty miles away. So I went to Reading South station, where the trains were green and Parliamentary (stopping everywhere), to catch the slow train. It was to be an oft repeated journey. I wandered up North Street beakily looking for the Co-op. Eventually I found the upstairs room and met Brian and Jean (9) who were pleased to offer a song and eventually, bless them, a bed for the night. I can't remember who the guest for the night was (possibly the Exiles) but I'd found a second home. If Ethnics was a slightly bohemian place to hone your skills (particularly after Bert

had gone – rusticated for quixotically tilting at the University's medieval sex laws), Guildford was Pandora's Box. Like many of the early folkies, Brian and Jean had been jazzers and skifflers. They were well connected on the London scene and knew both the Singers Club crowd and the team who ran the Fox in Islington. More than this they were traditional music nuts and not tolerant of anything less than the best. Tuesday was a good evening to fit in an extra gig for singers and musicians on tour from other parts of the country as well as for the up and comers from all over the south east. In the space of eighteen months I'd seen and heard, up close and personal, Seamus Ennis, the 4 Courts Ceilidh Band, Joe Heaney, Belle Stewart, Davie Stewart, Bert Lloyd, Charlie Bate and Mervyn Vincent, the Watersons and just about everyone else of about my own age who was making their way. We also used to see quite a bit of Reg Hall and the Rakes – my first introduction to the melodeon and the only good player of that wonderful instrument I was to encounter for many years

During the summer of 1964, my mate Dick (10) from Harrogate, now at Uni in Aberdeen asked if I'd like to come on a filming jaunt. Some bloke from the BBC was doing a documentary on the Battle of Culloden and they were looking for extras. Try keeping me away! Turned out that everyone bar the producer and the fight organiser were extras – one day a Redcoat, the next day a Clansman, though I never saw myself once through all the smoke of battle. But I did get to sing in the

Clansman Colin in 'Culloden', a docu-drama made in 1964 for the BBC, directed by Peter Watkins

Salvation Band

1. When I was just a little kid,
   On a Sunday morning early
   T' Salvation Band come down our street
   To make their hurly-burly.
   They all stood around in a great big ring
   And started blowin' t' cornets,
   And all the kids for miles around
   Come swarming up like hornets.
   Chorus: Salvation Band wi' the big trombone,
   And the music fair goes through yer,
   Wi' their "Onward Christian Soldiers"
   And their "Glory Hallelujah."

2. There were scores and scores and scores of kids,
   Perhaps there were even 30,
   And goodness knows who owned 'em all,
   But they all looked filthy dirty!
   There were Jackson's kid from across the street,
   And he were a reet young villain,
   T' collection box come round to him,
   He made off wi' 15 shillin'!

3. And t' man as stood and waved the stick
   Looked tall as half the houses,
   He'd got a brand-new uniform, wi'
   Wi' gold braid down the trousers!
   Behind him stood little Tommy Jones,
   Wi' his young grey pup called Rusty,
   And t' pup must've thought as t' man were a tree,
   'Cos t' gold braid's gone all rusty!

4. Now t' rest reckoned t' band weren't up to much,
   But me, I didn't mind 'em,
   So when they upped and marched away,
   I marched away behind 'em.
   We marched to t' other side of town,
   To streets I'd never been in,
   And we paused in t' yard o' t' public house,
   As me dad said I shouldn't be seen in!

5. Now when t' policeman fetched me home,
   They'd had their dinner wi'out me,
   And when me father found out where I'd been,
   I knew for a fact he'd clout me.
   Well I got t' buckle end o' me dad's pit-strap
   And that were plenty for me,
   I've never followed that band again
   And that's the end o' t' story!

'Salvation Band' by Roger Watson, written in his own fair hand Christmas 1964

film – my one and only time on the telly! The following autumn a young lad from Nottinghamshire turned up at Ethnics. He'd started to write songs drawing on tales from Notts and its mining traditions. One evening just after Christmas he said "Have a listen to this" and sang a song he'd just written called 'Salvation Band'. He of course was Roger Watson and much was to follow, a lot of it in London. I'd become intrigued by frequent references in the Melody Maker jottings to 'Three Rumbustuous Shantymen' and one night found a pub called the 'Scots Hoose', where downstairs there was a folk club. The three Shantymen turned out to be two men and a woman, one with a blond space age hairstyle and a voice to die for. I can't remember what I sang but the blond bloke went for it and shouted loudly "Good Man". I'd met Peter Bellamy, Royston Wood and Heather Wood, just forming as Young Tradition. Roger and I also started singing together a bit, but not all the time. He was becoming friendly with Eric Winter who published the folk magazine, 'Sing' and put several of Roger's songs in print, passing one – 'Christmas Hare' – on for a Roy Palmer book. Young Tradition were invited down to Ethnics and were mightily taken with Roger's 'Watercress-O' which they later recorded. Trips to London continued regularly and eventually when my course was over, I ended up with a job there.

Looking back, the London folk scene in 1965-66 was remarkable. From the single beginnings of the Ballads and Blues Club not much more than a decade earlier, Topsy had grown. Any night of the week, according to Melody Maker, there was a choice of ten or more venues in any folk style you might want. I tended to stay close to the 'Scots Hoose' (on Cambridge Circus, pub is now called the 'Spice of Life') where Bruce Dunnett, a craggy Scotsman put on a different show nearly every night. For a few short weeks Maddy Prior and Don Partridge on Monday, Bert Jansch on Tuesdays, Young Tradition on Sundays (I think!) and a guest who could be almost anyone on Friday. Round the corner was 'Bunjies' on Fridays, with Peter Bellamy and Al Stewart. Off in a different direction was 'Les Cousins', with mainly contemporary music, though it was a suitable place for the weekend insomniac. At the end of an evening you might find yourself in the Star, a Greek restaurant whose Spaghetti Neapolitan was a speciality, rubbing shoulders with who knows who. And less than a mile away was Colletts, wonderful Colletts Record Shop, where the ever supportive Hans Fried, himself very much part of the group of friends, would let you play anything – and there were wonders like the Dover edition of the 'Child Ballads' and Chappell's 'Popular Music of the Olden Time" littering the shelves, and anything you wanted about Russia and Socialism to buy. Perhaps it wasn't exactly a surprise just after the collapse of the Berlin Wall to come to London after a long absence and find that all the Colletts shops had just vanished.

Just to the north of the West End, in the village of Mount Pleasant stands a bloody great barn of a pub called 'New Merlins Cave'. Here the 'Singers Club' met every Saturday, hosted on alternate weeks by Bert Lloyd or Ewan MacColl and Peggy Seeger. Any youngster going for the first time must have felt they were entering hallowed ground. The Singers Club had broken from 'Ballads and Blues' some years earlier when its principals had recognised the need to accentuate British music in the face of the seemingly more popular American, but the principals were pivotal. On a Ewan and Peg night, they took the bulk of the time themselves unless a guest had been advertised. Nobody got to sing unless they were known – there was no singers list on the door – and that usually meant only members of McColl's own singer circle, the Critics Group got a song. But the place was like no other folk club I ever visited – it was full of men either in suits or working clothes, trade unionists all, communists most. I never went to the Singers Club without being drawn into

The Folk singer, Colin, in typical attitude

a conversation about the 1926 General Strike – forty years earlier. And there was a vast paradox. MacColl was a riveting singer, if very highly mannered (but who wasn't in those days?), and as good a songwriter as any in British popular music in the entire twentieth century. He was a captivating storyteller, with a comprehensive knowledge of traditional song and singers throughout the British Isles, He also had a genuine interest in patterns of speech of ordinary people which he wove carefully into his larger musical creations, particularly the Radio Ballads. He was a romantic without being either Arcadian or sentimentalist, and he had vast charisma. He was someone to admire, yet it was almost impossible for all but the very closest to him to love him, for in charge of a folk club he was a martinet, able to curdle the courage of the nervous or less than competent performer. His attempts to teach the world to sing folk songs in his own style were resented – most of the Critics Group singers were seen as identikit, whose singing lacked any personality other than Ewan's. What people knew of his origins, particularly his change of name in mid career gave rise to misunderstandings and jibes. His greatest strength, his left wing ideology born of a lifetime's experience was also his greatest weakness, as he was perceived as trying to create tradition, trying to establish a school of working class performing art in his own image. I can still remember some of the Festival of Fools shows in the winter – a mixture of Ewan's songs and some of the most biting satire I've ever heard. I admired him enormously – still do! Part of me would have loved to have joined the Critics Group – indeed I let this be known and might even have been welcome. But my individualistic liberal politics would not have lasted five minutes and so ....

Bert Lloyd's approach was subtler. Both Ewan and Bert knew they were part of an international movement creating and popularising working people's culture (the word class is being avoided) as a precursor to eventual political change. But Bert had worked in the Australian outback and on the Whaling Ships and had a pagan heart. He also recognised the Arcadian mentality that had informed the early twentieth century collectors as not being reflective of the whole English community, from whom the heritage of traditional folk song and music had come. He was anxious that what was handed on now, in the 1960s / 1970s, should look forward and should reflect the whole range of sources, not just the country ones. Over at least two decades he took every opportunity to feed songs to anyone who wanted them, particularly anyone who might popularise them in whatever style. He published two books ('Come all ye Bold Miners' and 'Folk Song in England') jointly authored the seminal 'Penguin Book of English Folk Songs', while LPs flowed out of Topic like water – industrial songs, sea songs, songs of magic and mystery – all supported by Bert's notes. Performers like Pentangle and Carthy and the Watersons grew repertoires quickly, partly through Bert's patronage and the old boy was not above whistling the odd tune out of the air – as the apocryphal story of him setting the ballad 'Jack Orion' to the tune of 'Donald Where's Your Trousers' illustrates.

The Fighting Cocks, Kingston upon Thames, a wonderful traditional club whose residents included Rod Stradling, Arthur Knevett, Pete Wood and Paddy Marchant

Did this matter? Did it matter that both Ewan and Bert were mixing what had been recovered from field singers (sometimes by them personally), with the great literary ballad collections of the nineteenth century, and with things they were creating themselves; songs they were writing, tunes they were inventing. Surely if a tradition is to grow it must be able to renew itself. It must resonate in the generation in which it is being presented, particularly amongst the young people of that generation. It must adapt to the musical genres and performance styles of that generation, almost certainly to its technology as well. It is a matter of history that Ewan and Bert achieved this – look at the discography of Pentangle particularly – the great ballads rose again from the printed page and entertained young people in the 1960s and 1970s. In an age of recorded music (and we have lived in one such at least since 1900 if you count written recording alongside sound and film), anything that is created is capable of being incorporated into an archive upon which the future can draw at any time. But Ewan and Bert energised the "now" of their time and created a mass movement out of next to nothing. More than that, they did it using songwriting, theatrical and publishing methods that directly mirror many of the conditions upon which the so called 'traditional' repertoire was created in the first place, between C16 and C19, before it passed into popular memory, and generations before the social parachutists we have come to know as folk song collectors recovered it from so called 'source singers'.

Little over a mile further north east from Mount Pleasant is Islington Green whose principal pub was in those days called The Fox. Here, on Thursday evenings, another of the great landmarks of the folk song revival emerged. Instantly recognisable as a business by the massive photographs of traditional performers (the one of Jimmy McBeath springs to mind) on all the walls, here Bob Davenport held court ably supported by the Rakes, Ernie Groome and Freddie McKay. Here the atmosphere was different. Traditional players were everywhere – mainly a host of Irish fiddlers, flute players etc, drawn in from sessions such as that at The Favourite in Holloway. Scan Tester was a regular visitor as was Jack Elliott of Birtley. While lip service was paid to folk music, traditional music was king here. The performers who were really valued were those who had been born to it in their families or grown up steeped in it within their communities. That's not to say that you weren't made welcome as an urban townie, but you knew instinctively that lots of people in this club thought you'd never be able to do it like Martin Byrnes or Margaret

Colin Cater and Roger Watson played the Folk Clubs together 1967-9

Barry. Although I enjoyed the music enormously, I was wary of the ideology – it seemed esoteric, Arcadian and very unreal in the middle of a large city. It seemed to be putting country before town (as Cecil Sharp had done) creating an inverted hierarchy of value in which it would be difficult, nigh impossible, for a young urban (dare I say middle class) singer to be assessed on equal terms with the 'real' country people. It was in short elitist.

One evening Bob announced that the club was issuing a special recording of country music players from East Anglia, in a limited edition of ninety nine records (this for legal reasons). I held back and didn't buy the thing until years later when Topic reissued it. I'd heard too many traditional 'old boys' who for all their country lineage didn't seem to have the musical skills to communicate effectively. In the process, I missed out on the formative stages of English Country Music – the tunes on this recording would provide both a repertoire and stylistic base for the English ceilidh dance music for the next decade or more. In time song clubs and indeed song itself would diminish as dance and music grew. Melodeons would abound everywhere, while young singers, particularly lads, would become as rare as hens teeth

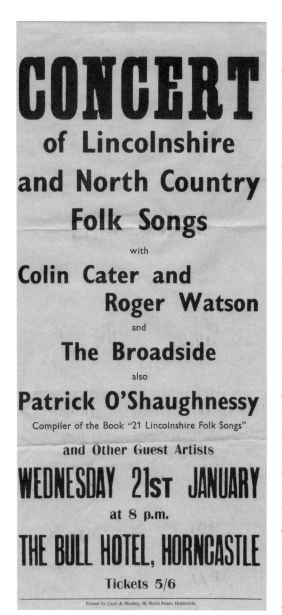

CONCERT

of Lincolnshire and North Country Folk Songs

with

Colin Cater and Roger Watson

and

The Broadside

also

Patrick O'Shaughnessy

Compiler of the Book "21 Lincolnshire Folk Songs"

and Other Guest Artists

WEDNESDAY 21ST JANUARY

at 8 p.m.

THE BULL HOTEL, HORNCASTLE

Tickets 5/6

Printed by Cupit & Hindley, 36, North Street, Horncastle.

For the moment, most of the singers who frequented the Scots Hoose and other central London venues looked at this developing argument and thought "A plague on both your houses". Young Tradition had a 'pad' in Kilburn which became a centre. Songs were practiced there and in the wonderful bathrooms of the tube station tunnels, where many of the ideas behind 'Lyke Wake Dirge', 'Byker Hill' and others first developed. If Peter was the perfect lead singer and Royston a wonderful bass line, Heather was one of the most imaginative harmonists I have ever heard, alternately singing counterpoints with either melody or bass to create stunning fusions. Success beckoned hard. For a brief moment we tried to set up a third London hub, somewhere for the younger singers who wanted to put distance between themselves and both Singers Club and Fox. We persuaded Ballet Rambert in Notting Hill to let us have their theatre on Wednesday evenings, and for just under three months we indulged ourselves, one of the many heroic artistic failures of the folk movement. We all knew that the movement needed the kind of leadership that would draw the different strands together. We were aware of EFDSS and Cecil Sharp House in Camden Town but the people who went there seemed as if they'd come from another planet (the planet Dance Earnestly). You might venture up there for the odd song evening, but the academic thing was for older people – singing the songs was what mattered, not finding out where they came from – so the Library was just a quiet room behind a large closed door. Much more memorable was the ill-fated attempt by Karl Dallas, the folk columnist of Melody Maker, to establish the 'London Folk Music Centre' in a Goodge Street cellar formerly used as a drinking club. It started as a great glory, clubs or concerts every evening, both book library and record library to browse through, wonderful singers – I still remember the only time I ever saw Doc Watson perform live. There were lots of opportunities for us to perform there ourselves, as long as we didn't want too much money. But the overheads were just too great – had it worked it would surely have become the folk equivalent to Ronnie Scott's – but in six months Karl had run out of money. However there is a personal post script. Karl immediately opened a Sunday evening club at the Adams Arms in Conway Street and all the young guns went to the first night to sing it in. During the evening I was introduced to Diane who became my partner for the next twenty years.

Four months later Diane and I landed in Nottingham for my one year PGCE, chosen in part because I'd got to know bits of it staying with Roger during vacations. Central Nottingham had two established clubs, both pretty eclectic, and a goodly collection of singers. MacColl and Lloyd had run an experimental folk theatre there several years previously, called 'Centre 42', where they had discovered Anne Briggs. One of the clubs, the 'Folk Scene' meeting on Fridays was about to change organiser – but the new organiser never settled to the task and three months later offered the venue to me. Initially taken aback, I reasoned that I was unlikely to be in Nottingham more than a few months, so set about creating a team who could run the club indefinitely into the future – there was Gil (11), his sister Pip (12), a young fresh faced lad called Paul (13) who was cutting a definite dash, and I also decided to approach Roy Harris whom I'd met some years earlier when Roger booked him as a guest at Ethnics (Roger, studying German, was on the overseas year of his degree). Roy lived just outside Nottingham and had no time for the Nottingham clubs. We agreed to meet in my flat, but I had not anticipated the extensive 'manifesto' that Roy would bring with him – all about singing songs from our own country only, and if possible from our own locality. Adopting it was easy; it was the view of tradition we all really believed in. We thought there might be a few ripples in Nottingham, but there were plenty of other clubs locally for the mid-Atlantically inclined. We didn't anticipate either the degree of support we got in Nottingham itself or the rumblings this manifesto would cause around the country for years to come. So, on January 29th 1967, 'Nottingham Traditional Music Club' (the NTMC) was born – quite the best folk club it was ever my privilege to be involved with. We weren't bigots either – the first two guests were Hope Howard (a young West Indian lad living in Nottingham) and Tom Paley from USA.

Invitation to the recording gig at NTMC

Tupton Hall School in Derbyshire provided me with my first job eight months later – without a car Nottingham might just as well have been Australia. There were a lot of good clubs, young singers and musicians just starting out in Derbyshire, soon to be movers and shapers (John Tams, Keith Kendrick, Johnny Adams, Mick Peat were all young lads). I also got to know Frank Sutton, an older chap who was an expert on gothic Derbyshire ballads and ran a weekly informal singaround at the Yellow Lion in Chesterfield. Roger was back in England too and

> **Colin Cater and Roger Watson**
> request the pleasure of the company and vocal dexterity of
>
> ....
>
> **at a Recording Session**
>
> to be held at the
> N.T.M.C., 'The News House,' St. James' Street (near City centre)
> Nottingham
>
> on ....November, 1969
>
> at 7.30 pm
>
> Session to be supervised by Bill Leader
>
> RSVP to

soon afterwards we started to gig. Roy got us a spot on a concert in Stoke-on-Trent and the club booked us in soon afterwards. Having only sung solo unaccompanied before, working with someone else offered freedoms undreamed of. With harmonies, and the chance to sing with Roger's guitar or English Concertina accompaniments, it became possible to communicate with people in significant numbers. What followed was a bit of a whirlwind. We decided to hustle for gigs in teacher training colleges and had instant take up. Folk clubs as far spread as London, Worcester, Lincolnshire, Newcastle all came in. Personally I remember Pete Coe's club in Birmingham, Horncastle, Malvern, Crewe, Gloucester, Cheltenham, South Shields, Leeds and others with enduring pleasure while 'Baxter's Night Club' in Bishop Auckland remains unique in its awfulness. We were approached by Bill Leader to do a record, largely thanks to Eric Winter's influence, and having decided to do it live set up two sessions in NTMC's room with audience invited. Then the world fell in; we had two or three major disagreements and one night on the way back from a gig in London Roger said he wanted to pack it in.

COLIN CATER and Roger Watson, Clay Cross folk singers, rehearse for their new record album.

CLAY CROSS SINGERS WHO DIG THOSE MINING DITTIES

By a staff reporter

COAL and beer will feature strongly on a record album to be made by two well-known Clay Cross folk singers, Roger Watson and Colin Cater.

Both believe the songs of the mining areas of Derbyshire, Nottinghamshire and the West Riding have been neglected on records compared with those of other regions, like Northumberland and Durham.

"To get a real folky atmosphere we've decided to record live before an invited audience in a Nottingham Folk Club on November 11 and 12 with plenty of local accents," said Colin.

CHORUS

Roger added: "More than half of the songs are chorus numbers, and we will need a lively audience."

The duo first met at Reading University and they teamed up in February last year.

Both are teachers, Colin at Tupton Hall Comprehensive School, Clay Cross; and Roger at Breaston, near Long Eaton.

Between three and five songs will be Roger's own compostions.

GERMAN

"One features a watercress seller who visited the mining villages in Nottinghamshire until the 1926 strike in my grandmother's day," he said.

Another is an English translation made by him of a German folk song while studying in Germany.

Two Derbyshire songs collected by Dronfield folk singer Frank Sutton will also be featured.

Colin added: "It should be a rousing record." They play between them a guitar, melodeon, concertina, and whistle as well as sing.

Shortly before the split, Colin & Roger appear in the Sheffield evening newspaper, The Star

The record never came out. Looking back, with all the disappointment consigned to history, he was right. I may have been a good harmony lead and solo singer, but Roger played all the instruments and wrote a goodly part of our repertoire (I'd just contributed a couple of tunes, including 'No. 2 Top Seam'). Roger also did all the driving and had to put up with the endless thoughts of Chairman Colin. By the time we split there were songs he'd written that he was refusing to sing because he was totally sated with them – a scenario that would overtake me personally in time. If he was knackered and thought there was more to life than folk clubs and cars, who could blame him – the rest of his career stands as testament to his very considerable talent and individuality. We remain friends to this day. My life had also changed. I knew by then for certain that there was no living for me to be made through folk music – a glorious hobby yes, but occupation, no. I had two kids and wanted to get out of both comprehensive schools and teaching History very much. It was time to move on again and to finally end my adolescence. I was 27.

Almost by chance, I got a job in Chelmsford. The local folk club was in the 'Three Cups'. Roger and I had gigged there and knew the local singers were very good – particularly Nic Jones. It was a concert club, which reduced me to a bit player, difficult after three years gigging. The guest list was pretty stunning, but that wasn't the main reason why people came in their hundreds. It was of course, Nic, arguably the best and most inventive guitarist and singer the English folk music movement ever produced (Martin Carthy notwithstanding). I'd met Nic earlier and knew one of his obsessions was finding ways to make a primarily rural music from times past accessible to young people in towns and cities today. He'd imbibed all the MacColl strictures about accompaniment not detracting from the primacy of the song, but he wasn't about to burn his guitar as others did – quite the reverse he gradually

Chelmsford Folk Club band, drumming up support in the town centre
l to r – Mick & Sarah Graves, Mel McGann, Colin, Steve Morris, Howard Jones & 'an audient'

extended the range of accompaniment devices used, but always to underscore the song itself. He saw the guitar as an essential part of the technology of his environment, whose use would better enable him to communicate with young people whose primary cultural experience was mainstream. What I didn't realise until years later was quite how many of the melodies he used he had written himself, or the extent to which he was renewing the tradition himself.

By the mid 1970s, although we didn't realise it, the first flush of the folk song club movement was all but over and its geography almost set. Nearly all the generation of performers who would illuminate the movement for the next four decades was active by the mid 1970s. A stream of books and records had made the folk repertoire widely and easily accessible. However, change was afoot. Folk dance was about to enjoy a great boom, both Morris and ceilidh dancing. The locus of the movement was also starting to move from the Club to the Festival. Pubs were themselves changing. Walls were being knocked down, restaurants opened and upstairs rooms closed. It was the era of Watney's. In time, as pop music changed and punk, then rap and dance culture came in, the clear link between pop styles and (some) folk styles would be broken and the supply of young people into the folk clubs would diminish to a trickle. Folk would become a separate musical genre, more of a counter culture than it had been in the glory years of the clubs. As folk performers became more mature, perhaps creativity also took a back seat to skill development. I staggered on as a solo singer, unable to find anyone else I wanted to sing with, doing the occasional club gig, but the combination of splitting from Roger and relocating from Derbyshire to Essex probably had a greater effect on me than I realised, particularly it would be years before the pointlessness of singing about coal pits and cotton mills to the good folk of Billericay finally dawned – without industry whence lay my integrity as a singer? Possibly in other parts of social history, possibly in country sports and pursuits, certainly in songs about the great people's heroes of history, Wolfe, Nelson, Benbow and the great sea battles of centuries past. Although I didn't realise it in 1970, singing for me was to enter a fallow period that would last for a very long time.

Friends mentioned in this section
1   Robin Dransfield
2   The Crimple Mountain Boys:
      (Robin & Barry Dransfield, Roger Knowles, Dave Brailsford and Pete Gallagher)
3   Rennie Pickles
4   Dave Brady
5   Martin Cummins
6   John Pashley who sung regularly with Dennis Sabey, who ran the Bradshaw Tavern
7   Boris Howarth aka Bert Worth (as I knew him)
8   Brian and Jean Dunt who ran Guildford Folk Club for many years
9   Bob and Carole Pegg
10   Dick Muir
11   Gil Harper
12   Pip Harper
13   Paul Golding

Those Dancing Years

Despite best intentions, adolescence died hard. Within three years I'd become one of the founders of Chelmsford Morris and with several mates formed the ceilidh band Lumps of Plum Pudding, setting a pattern for the next two decades. At some point the melodeon hove into view and the never ending struggle to try to play the thing just a little bit better. Progress was painfully slow. Morris tunes were a godsend, but my family's ears must have bled. I'd just started to tinker with accompanying songs on a melodeon when I picked up an Anglo Concertina (a Jefferies, no less) in a junk shop, and then had another one built by Colin Dipper. Morris became central to the social calendar, a seemingly endless stream of "Fetes worse than Death" including even a couple of Fetes when we won the Tug of War, then Lumps started gigging merrily, creating tensions all round and making me wonder how any of us ever found time to go to work.

I'd joined EFDSS and quickly but briefly found my way on to its committees. For a couple of years I became involved with the organisational side of both Sidmouth and Whitby Festivals. In the early 1970s, folk festivals were gearing up largely through the initiative of EFDSS through its field staff, particularly Bill Rutter. I was never quite sure why I was asked to run the singing at Sidmouth for two years, but Bill agreed instantly that every opportunity should be taken to break down barriers between song and dance. Things were different then. Budgets were smaller; booked guests fewer and venues far more informal. But there was a seemingly unending stream of very talented young people wanting nothing more than free tickets and the chance to strut their stuff. The principal Sidmouth song venue, the 'Beach Store' was run like a folk club with three sessions a day, some of them themed. Anyone could sing if they got their names on the list early enough, but the MCs were primed to fit the good up-and-coming singers in and give them slightly longer spots (three or four songs instead of two). This was how I first heard June Tabor, Pete and Chris Coe, John Kirkpartick (then a musician only), Songwainers, Vin Garbutt and many others. Every attempt was made to incorporate dancers into these sessions, although space was a problem. Lots of Morris sides came down every year and danced on the streets, which must have rather overwhelmed the long standing Festival sides in Festival Dress – remember the 'felt skirt brigade' (only with a shudder). Evening Late Night Extra shows were also just starting up, going on for hours into the night until one year the locals complained. Lovely memories of Taffy's Magic Lantern Show (13), of 'Black

Jefferies Anglo concertina – a junk shop find

'Essex Occassionals' win the Tug-O-War at Dartmoor Festival 1986
l to r – Colin, Don Waugh, Simon Ritchie, ?, Joyce Hollowbread, ?, Julia Landsman, Peter Billinge, Phil Heath-Coleman

Lumps of Plum Pudding in the procession at Sidmouth Folk Festival 1974
l to r – Colin, Mick & Sarah Graves, Mel McGann, Bill Delderfield

and White Morris' – a side of coppers dancing Bean Setting using their truncheons for sticks, and I was told years afterwards that I'd been the first person to put Women's Morris on the stage at Sidmouth in the shape of the compelling England's Glory.

Gradually however my focus of interest became more localised – there always seemed to be a tension between having a national reputation and being penniless on the one hand and entertaining people locally and having a few quid in your pocket afterwards on the other. For twenty years as band musician and then caller, I chose the latter. Over the next decade 'Lumps' did Sidmouth a few times and other Festivals as well but after English Country Music emerged we were never leading edge. However we were booked in at the Earl of Rone revels at Combe Martin, North Devon two or three times, my first up close exposure to a folk custom. The Earl was a revival after an interval of more than a century, put together by North Devon folkies, particularly Tom and Barbara Brown from very detailed contemporary C19 descriptions of the Earl, Obby Oss and Teaser and Grenadiers. It was a weekend of processions, based on local legend of the shipwreck and capture of the Earl of Tyrone following his flight from Ulster in the early C17 – a total fabrication but very picturesque and hiding who knows what in older meaning. But it didn't feel like a re-enactment. Up close to the surging drumbeat, swaying dancing, regular ceremonial executions of the Earl and liberal supplies of sloe gin this was other worldly, a spiritually uplifting experience, a chance for a good sing and a bloody good grin too! Seed corn was sown and though I wasn't able to go all that often, the experience was to be repeated participating in other customs.

Colin as the 'Oss at –

Hunting the Earl of Rone, Combe Martin, North Devon 1997

I can't let this section pass without special mention of the wonderful Greg Trice, who arrived unexpectedly in Chelmsford Morris quite early on. Coming from a musical background as a pianist and church organist, he was just about the only Englishman living south of Durham that I ever heard play the piano accordion crisply. He also took up the Jefferies Duet concertina – an instrument that requires

a double first in Maths merely to understand. A genuine eccentric he simply didn't recognise boundaries – rules existed to be challenged. All right,' play music within established conventions if that is what's needed for people to dance to it, but why shouldn't a hornpipe be in 5: 4 time? Over the next few years he wrote a series of bizarre tunes – splendid melodies but impossible on the melodeon unless you were a very good player and had at least a two and a half row instrument. Together we formed an unlikely nucleus around which 'Lumps of Plum Pudding' (14) was formed – and he got me writing. Working with Roger it had seemed that there was a natural order – things he could do that I couldn't, like singing harmonies and writing songs and tunes. Greg's tune making had the opposite effect; it was a spur needing a response. The desire to emulate his 'Moulsham Street Hornpipe' and 'Danbury Hill' found me in my front room one Saturday, melodeon over shoulder, so that in about half a day three jigs emerged of my very own make, conveniently in keys of D, E minor and G. 'Lumps' used them for years for 'Circassian Circle', under the collective title of 'General Amin's Retreat (from sanity)'. More than that, it was somehow fixed that they won a tune competition at Sidmouth and were broadcast live on Folk on Two. Greg himself was like a supernova – a research scientist, he packed his job in because his company wouldn't give him free rein and suddenly he was gone. He emigrated to Canada, where in the absence of an active folk scene he composed several orchestral pieces based around English folk tunes like Orange and Blue, which though preformed in Canada have never been aired in England, their true home. He died very prematurely in 1993.

During the 1970s and 1980s, in addition to Cotswold Morris with Chelmsford and playing for barn dances, I got involved in all sorts of other things. From the very first Chelmsford Morris Men 'summer season' it was clear that a social problem

Chelmsford Morris in Border kit at Rendham, Suffolk, 1976
l to r – back row – Bob Etheridge, Jim Etheridge, Dave Shields, Ken May, John Parsons, Alan Cottrill, Kieran Fitzgerald, Derek Gerring (Ern), Martin Bates, Pete Harding, front row – Bob Sawyer, Steve Monk, Colin Cater, Clive Taylor

existed finding something for the women to do in what seemed like an all male pastime. Luckily the opportunity arose to plug into initiatives being developed elsewhere and the girls got involved first with step clog and then later North West Morris. Naturally gender politics kicked in but Chelmsford resolved matters by removing the 'Men' from their name, and becoming two sides of equal status. However my Morris interest started to wane as 'North West' music seemed just too regimented. For me the glory of playing for Morris is in Cotswold, forming an empathy with the movements of dancers and as far as possible tailoring playing to the needs of individuals. Border Morris (Chelmsford danced this mainly in the winter) was fun though and much better for keeping warm. As far as possible Chelmsford stuck to the collected Border repertoire and didn't invent their own dances, a pattern which was to repeat itself when the Good Easter Molly Gang got going – only twice a year, Plough Monday and Whittlesea Straw Bear (until very recently) – a chance to dance the traditional dances from our own part of the country. Eventually, the search for a bit more of a musical challenge led me away from Chelmsford to join the rapper team Hoddesdon Crownsmen, which also kept me in touch with what was happening nationally, particularly through the folk festivals.

Looking back, we were all both individuals and part of a collective whole. A couple of starlings feeding in a back garden seem obvious individuals, but soaring, wheeling and turning in echelon of several thousand they become part of a much larger entity. So with folk, the experiences of this young singer were replicated all over the country; similarly with Morris. Large numbers of people found Morris through the folk clubs over quite a short time – first Cotswold, and then as curiosity grew, the other Morris genres, then customs and ceilidh dancing. More curiously many of the tensions that had developed in song also emerged in Morris. Should traditional forms be used or should new forms be created based on what had happened in the past? Definitions were slightly different. Traditional Morris was seen as what had been collected mainly by Cecil Sharp from Cotswold villages. For some it was paramount to give the best interpretations possible of the recovered material and nothing else was acceptable as Morris (although this didn't always extend to watching and copying the style of teams like Bampton, whose Morris tradition had continued to evolve through C20) The proscription of women dancing by the Morris Ring was justified in traditional terms. For others the Ring and its rampant sexism was anathema. More than this, the traditional repertoire for Border, Molly, North West simply wasn't extensive enough for many teams who created their own dances in a wonderful creative outflow based on adapting the old styles to a contemporary environment, totally untouched by contemporary mass media – a situation conforming to many definitions of 'traditional process'. Sadly Morris gender politics also created a fault line, institutionalised by the emergence of three separate Morris organisations.

Throughout the 1970s Chelmsford Folk Song Club continued in pretty lively fashion although by 1980 the best venues in the town were all but used up and the less formal 'session' was starting to take over – more music than song and with less need for quiet and order. I'd continued writing a bit, only tunes, particularly the 'Tricky Dicky' and 'Liberation' Polkas. Then one week, someone bet me that I couldn't write a song by the following week, and it got me going. The next week I turned up with a comic song about one of our friends (this song now thankfully consigned to the dustbin of history). A little while later, following the lead of

Colin playing for Good Easter Molly Gang – dancing 'Special Molly' outside 'The Plough', Little Downham, Cambs. Ouse Washes day of dance, January 2009, l to r – dancers: Ken Baker, Paul Reece, Dick Peacock,Geoff Walker (back), Neil Munro, Simon Ritchie, Music: Dave Ponting, Ray Clarke(elbow), Colin, Fred Field

another Essex songwriter, Jim Garrett, who'd been inspired, by something he saw in the car park at his local railway station, to write the song 'Flat Battery', I wrote another song, 'Change at Thorpe-le-Soken' and for some reason this caught people's imagination. Was it because it was modelled on East Anglian comic songs like 'The Fella that played the Trombone' or because you couldn't stand on a railway station anywhere east of London without hearing the mantra "Change at Thorpe-le-Soken for Walton on the Naze"? Very soon I couldn't go anywhere without being asked for it, which made me feel good for a while before wearing a bit thin. But it was years before it was anything other than a one hit wonder.

After ten years I decided to leave Lumps of Plum Pudding. It had been enormous fun but we had overworked and I was very stale – when you start looking at people enjoying themselves to your music, and then start wondering how can this be when you're bored out of your skull, it's time to move on. Looking back, Bill Delderfield's ability to insult people and still make them laugh was remarkable, so much so that afterwards I decided to become a caller, for the next ten years or so working with as many different bands as possible, mainly for PTAs, sports clubs and an almost infinite number of weddings. Although I kept contact with 'the folk movement', in the main I worked outside its bounds, operating in a world of occasional participants rather that inside a movement of committed enthusiasts. But there was no doubting that these occasional participants enjoyed the folk music they were offered considerably. A lot of the same faces kept turning up at barn dances, not folkies but people with fully active lives who would come to a barn dance twice or three times a year and have a hell of a lot of fun, then resume their life patterns without being involved with 'folk' at all, until the next time. A weekend festival for many barn dance goers would have been absolute overkill. How also does anyone explain a pub full of noisy drinkers when the folk band is on – they don't want to listen at all, but they do want to hear the music and be part of the ambience – this happened every Sunday night in Chelmsford for years. The pub would have been empty if the musicians hadn't been there, but listen, no, not on your life. It was on one such sainted occasion in at the end of 1992 that Karen and I first met – she ran the gauntlet of noise and sang 'Green Fields of Canada', a song I hadn't heard for years – in a pub in Chelmsford? – this woman had to be very special!

Hoddesdon Crownsmen dance at Karen and Colin's wedding, Chapel & Wakes Colne Steam Railway museum, July 1995
l to r – Snowy as the 'Tommy', Richard Sissons, Gareth Ford, Alan Collins, Tom Bending, Martin Hirst, Ken Arton as the 'Betty'

By the time Karen and I met, my feelings about the folk movement had become very ambivalent: I loved the music, but had all sorts of reservations about how I perceived the mainstream thinking driving it to be. Whatever might be achieved locally by barn dance bands and Morris teams, it seemed that the folk movement nationally hadn't really got any strategies for reaching out to non-enthusiasts, despite being quite a substantial industry in its own right. As a youngster it had taken me several years to make the

Lumps of Plum Pudding – *l to r Bill Delderfield (Caller), Clive Taylor, Colin, Mel McGann, Gordon Folkard (now better known as Anahata), Micky Graves*

transition from pop music fan to folkie, this in an era (the 1960s / 70s) when there were obvious bridges (Skiffle, the Dubliners, Steeleye Span) between the two genres. By the early 1990s, when the youngsters of the 1960s had become the movement's leaders, it seemed as if they had forgotten their own transitional years, and that much of the movement felt like a large circle with everyone linking arms and facing inwards rather than outwards towards the world, an unfortunate situation with the gulf between mainstream pop and folk culture now so much wider. Could this have happened because the folk movement was founded on an esoteric separatist ideology (that of Cecil Sharp et al) never overturned despite all the work of McColl and Lloyd? I hankered for an ideology that was inclusive: of urban as well as rural origins; of literate as well as unlettered sources; of the technology of the current time as well as of times past; of the cultures of all British people; of recently created material alongside the collections of several generations ago. It seemed that quasi-academic Folk societies particularly the Folk Song Society / EFDSS / Morris Ring, in the interests of preservation had frozen tradition in time, in both repertoire and stylistic terms. What they had assembled was a written musical archive of C19 vernacular song and dance, which was only part of a much larger archive of the whole history of English / British vernacular music. It seemed that the latter day inheritors of the collections were clinging to them as if they were still alive, and strangling them further in the process, rather than using them as a basis for future growth using the technology and skills of 'now'. Come back creativity – both song and Morris revolutions of the 1960s and 1970s were founded on it, as well as on the collections. I was also set on two other things: as musically English folk was what I was steeped in, this would be the medium I would use for any future creative activity; in the light of experience I would in future also always try to look at folk culture holistically – the social conditions which gave rise to the recovered song repertoire were broadly the same as those in which Morris Dancing flourished, or Sword Dancing, Country Dancing, Mumming Plays, clog dancing, local customs the list is as long as folk activity itself. Meeting Karen was

FOR A NICE TASTY SOUND!

LUMPS OF PLUM PUDDING

CALLER: BILL DELDERFIELD

CHRISTMAS REUNION CEILIDH

SATURDAY 16th DECEMBER

at Mill Hall Rayleigh 8pm 'til Midnight

TICKETS £4.50 *including omnivorous buffet*

From Sarah: 0621 853941   Colin: 0245 355019

Bill: 0702 353020

ALL PROCEEDS TO PETER DASHWOOD

Poster design – Sarah Graves

The Church Band

l to r – Roy Nicholls, Sam Bond, Jeff Giddings, Mick & Sarah Graves, Tony Roberts, Paul McCann, Peter Booth, Jill Palmer-Swift

Wedding procession

wonderfully timely. I was ready for another tilt at the windmill, and particularly to start singing seriously again.

Eighteen months later, in July 1995, Karen and I were married, on a glorious summer's day, with our friends doing the music as a Church Band and everyone singing like St Peter's Braintree had run a folk club for years, then in the evening dancing to 'Saturday Night' (15) and Bill Delderfield, easily my favourite ceilidh band and caller ever. Quite how life changing things were to become was not yet apparent. For the moment music was the principal interest we shared. Karen had been a folkie for a long time. In the 1970s she'd packed up a boring Graphic Design course in Norwich to go gigging and dossing round Germany for a year with a band of mad Irishmen called 'The Wild Geese', playing bodhran and singing, both of which she did splendidly. On her return to England, gainful employment called and she worked as principal designer to an internationally recognised glass engraving company in Norfolk and disappeared from the folk music arena completely. By the

time she came to live in Essex, she had two kids and paid artwork was confined to occasional commissions and the odd exhibition, though there was no mistaking either her talent or the unusual insights she could throw on subject material. She came back into folk almost by accident, though the muse was already calling, stumbling on a weekly session in a pub only a couple of hundred yards from home. But the old hooks were strong; she started to go to Chelmsford sessions regularly and so it was we met a couple of years later.

*l to r –
Aly Mewse,
Colin Cater,
Karen (Mewse)
Cater*

Although folk music had been Karen's passion as well as mine, the paths we had trodden had been very different. She knew very little of traditional music in England and almost nothing of Morris Dancing (ah! what bliss!). We went first to the jolly local session at the Compasses, Littley Green, run by the oft lamented Monkey (Steve Monk), where step dancing and East Anglian melodeon playing were highly valued, along with everything else offered. From there it was a relatively short step to the National Festival at Sutton Bonnington where the great and good of the traditional music world congregated every year and then into the summer festivals, particularly Whitby. I also took Karen to the Earl of Rone at

Monday night session at the Compasses, Littley Green
l to r – Keith Cilvert, Monkey (Gaffer, Steve Monk) playing melodeon and step dancing, Colin playing Dipper Anglo concertina

Combe Martin, having not been myself for over a decade, and to the Abbots Bromley Horn Dance in early September.

Little by little we started to build up both a performing repertoire and a passion for customs. Because her voice was pitched quite high, she suggested I might sing bass line harmonies – incredibly difficult at first having spent a lifetime believing I couldn't do it.

Karen worked on her banjo playing, and then one Sunday I was offered a melodeon keyed in Bb and Eb that sounded like a fairground organ and was perfect to accompany Karen's voice. One or two gigs came but we really had a lot of work to do, and in any case we'd decided to concentrate on opening our own club (bloody silly thing to do – everyone else was closing them). A year after we married the 'Essex Singers Club' was born, in the atmospheric surroundings of Chappel and Wakes Colne railway station, with the local enthusiasts providing the bar, and different ale each time. We'd gathered a team of people to form the resident nucleus – Robin & Gill (17) and Chris (18) – and we hoovered up good ideas from almost anywhere we could find them: three halves; shorter guest spots to get lots of singers on; silly raffle prizes; passing the wassail bowl at

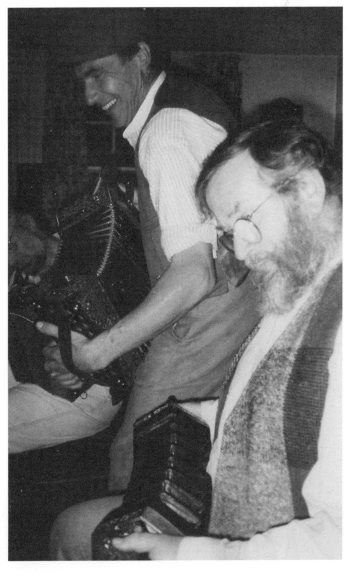

CASTLE CAMPS COCK-UP AT STEAMFOLK
8th March 1997

our winter party; strawberries and cream in high summer, and of course the best and most varied guest list we could put together. It was superb. We stayed with it for three years, until our circumstances had changed and we knew we couldn't stay on without becoming absentee landlords. But the Club had become a community; talk to people a decade later or close your eyes and the memories still crowd in – mention . . . well almost anyone who was there at the time.

It was when we'd been married for two years that the opportunity arose to retire from gainful employment and to strike out on our own. We spent a summer wallowing in new found freedom and wondering how we would ever fill our lives, before deciding to develop an enterprise based around Karen's artistic talents. We eventually settled on the name 'Hedingham Fair' and our early experiences are set out in the next section. Needless to say we made lots of mistakes – the biggest of which was to assume that depicting folk culture artistically would lead to its being taken up by the general public. We spent the summer of 1998 and part of 1999 showing our wares at a combination of local craft fairs, national trade fairs and folk events before realising conclusively that only the folk events were working. If we wanted to sell we would have to travel to Folk Festivals and other large events where other people who shared our passions gathered

By the turn of the Millennium, 'Hedingham Fair' had been going several years and had become a way of life for both of us – designing time in the winter, spring and early summer, Festivals in May, then again in the late summer and early autumn, mail order in the last three months of the year – all the time rubbing shoulders with exactly the people and activities we knew we'd wanted to be part of all our lives. In the end, there wasn't time for gigging in the performance sense, but our whole lives were a gig. Should we feel the need for some music or singing, a good session within an hour's drive was only a couple of days away at most. Oh, and just as a postscript, in 2003 I accepted the invitation to join Thaxted Morris Men – themselves an institution after nearly a hundred years of history. Out of this wonderful environment much if not all of Karen's art has come – all firmly rooted in the folklore and traditions of the land. So too have come my songs and tunes, building culturally on a line of English musical development traceable back centuries. I'd like to think these songs might become part of the natural heritage of the broadside and theatrical song making traditions of centuries past, and that they might in time become part of cultural England. But that's for the future isn't it.

Opposite – One memorable night when the regulars of the monthly session at Castle Camps 'Cock' hired a bus and came to Essex Singers Club, christened "Steamfolk" by Monkey (*Steve Monk*) *playing harmonica and dancing a Jig-doll top r and centre left, also polka-ing bottom left with wife Marilyn also present: Neil Lanham – step dancing top l & centre l, polka-ing bottom l with wife Hazel; Chris Manners – guitar bottom r; next – Robin Carpenter – melodeon, then Gill Mariner – banjo; Marilyn & Merrilyn step clogging; Jack Tarling (singer) in flat hat seated centre r; Alan Hardy & Ken Hunnybun (Bitter End shanty singers) top l; Arthur, land lord of 'Cock', Colin, Jim Jones-Williams, Gill & ? playing swannee whistles and kazoos won in the raffle upper centre r.*

Karen & Colin Cater performing at Essex Singers Club March 2000, by then moved to the Rayleigh Arms, Terling

Poster design – Karen Cater

Friends mentioned in this section

14   Taffy Thomas.

15   Lumps of Plum Pudding: initially Colin – melodeon, Greg Trice – Piano
Accordion, Mick Graves – fiddle, Clive Taylor – banjo and Mel McGann –
bass, with Bill Delderfield calling. After Greg left: Gordon Folkard (now
better known as Anahata) – Piano Accordion, then Sarah Graves –
English Concertina; Much later Peter Booth – guitar.

16   Saturday Night: Ed Caines – fiddle, Colin Handley – trumpet, Chris Beal –
Jeffries Duet Concertina and Joanne Pooley – Piano.

17   Robin & Gill Carpenter.

18   Chris Manners.

**Hedingham Fair
stall
Chippenham
Folk Festival
2008**

The Contexts in which the Songs are set

Ever since my partnership with Roger Watson in the late 1960s, I've always fancied myself as a bit of a tunesmith, although it's been some time since many of the early tunes saw the light of day – somewhere in my shelves lays a manuscript book full of pieces put together during my ceilidh band time, to provide the band with some of its repertoire. The notion of writing song words didn't really take hold until the late 1970s – partly as the result of a bet during a pub session. Most of the early songs were a bit wordy and political, but clearly this has changed since Karen and I met, married and set up Hedingham Fair to design and produce greetings cards and T-shirts, and sell books and gifts, all with folk themes. Now music making usually takes the form of doodling – sitting, melodeon in hand, in the kitchen next to the stove letting melodies come out; and then evaporate on the air. Some tunes survive long enough to get played in sessions and several of the song melodies are included in this collection. Sometimes a set of words will be put together: either these will come in a great rush, or alternatively ideas will waft on the wind for a very long time before finally taking shape. Some of the inspiration comes from other people's catch phrases. 'Change at Thorpe' and 'Steam with Santa' both happened in this way, but inspiration for many of them has come from what Karen and I do – somehow it's a very short step from producing images about Wassailing, Mumming

In his usual place, Colin playing by the stove

or Molly Dancing to writing songs about them. As for style, well I've sung traditional songs for several decades now, so I could hardly suddenly start writing rock 'n' roll. In any case the old styles have grandeur about them that I can't help but love – it's time they made a comeback as part of living tradition, and if this small collection can assist, wouldn't that be good.

Establishment of Hedingham Fair in 1997 changed Karen's and my lives in several ways. Commuting and the home / work dislocation disappeared completely, along with pointless meetings and the need to conform to the agenda of others. Our work is now our life, indeed a way of life. Folk music and culture, until then a thread running separately through both our lives, suddenly became their fulcrum, although we didn't see immediately where this might lead. With others we set up a song club, retracing steps into one of the most rewarding phases of my life. Hedingham Fair also presented an opportunity to put into practice the notion of linking all the different aspects of folk culture holistically – to be able to celebrate song and singers, with Morris and dancers, as well as Mummers and those who in their own communities took part in annual customs celebrations, some of whom were folkies at other times of the year and some not so.

In 1997, the year of liberation from gainful employment we produced a series of six greetings cards. We both knew that Karen had a very real artistic talent and that if we didn't seek to harness it now the chance would probably not come again. Applying it to the music and culture we both loved was easy. Karen preferred to work in relief mainly as a lino cutter, so we bought a printing press and decided to develop a set of images based mostly on East Anglian customs. To an already existing Mummers Play image 'Old Father Christmas', were added 'Bold St George', 'Wassailing', the 'Cutty Wren' (Middleton, Suffolk), 'Molly Dancing' and one of the Bear and Keeper from the incomparable 'Whittlesea Straw Bear'. The Molly image of Old Glory Molly Dancers which included the legend "Only once a year, Penny for the Ploughboys", quickly became a star, but the overall idea was well received in the folk movement, particularly at festivals, so much so that we began to wonder if the designs might have currency outside the folk community in the wider world. Eventually we would learn that there were just too many barriers for this to happen.

Thaxted Morris Men dance 'Balance the Straw' outside Thaxted Guildhall, at the meeting of the Morris Ring 2008
Dancers l to r: Ian Anderson, Mike Wilkinson, Cliff Marchant in top hat, Geoff Walker, Daniel Fox; Music: Colin, Simon Ritchie; under the Guildhall is Hedingham Fair's stall

Partly influenced by my ambivalence to folk orthodoxy, we decided to concentrate on those aspects of tradition that were in current performance and celebration. Images of other customs followed but we deliberately avoided sentimental events like the centenary of Cecil Sharp's first encounter with William Kimber (1999). However important and formative the past might be we told ourselves "Tradition is Now", and that this is what we would attempt to illustrate. On this basis we could comfortably encompass the notion of constant modification and change – we quickly learned that Customs could be subdivided between those that had been celebrated constantly since time immemorial, those whose celebration had been restarted after a (sometimes very long) time gap, and those created in modern times. It would also enable us to recognise the changing nature of UK society and celebrate occasions sacred and special to the newer communities for whom Britain had become home. When in 2000, someone suggested that we might produce a Calendar, and the 'Calendar of Traditional Customs' came into being we were able to do just this – list religious and secular celebrations irrespective of origin. We also squeezed out as many of the errors as we could find passed down through generations of copied books and internet sites – this was a lengthy process and we owe a debt of gratitude to the folk 'tourists' who provided good humoured feedback often after our Calendar had misled them (thanks guys!). The Calendar quickly developed an established format with an illustration, a piece of potted folklore (written from my own nonconformist standpoint) and as many events as possible listed for every month, with a front cover illustration combining the customs usually form a particular part of the year (1).

For the moment it seemed possible to sideline many of the issues about which the 'so called' folk intelligentsia seemed exercised and on which I regularly found myself holding an opposing viewpoint: was folk music the music of the country or of the whole community; should oral transmission be pre-eminent or greater value be placed on printed sources; how significant is continuousness of tradition; is folk transmission of greater value when located within individual families; is folk expression the milieu solely of working class people or the whole community. There was one issue we were unable to ignore – that of belief (please reader note, not religion).

In the last century or so the attitude of academic folklore towards non-Christian origins of folk customs has undergone a complete pendulum swing. Following the lead established in C19 by Frazer et al (2), Cecil Sharp embraced the ideas of folk customs etc. having Pagan origins or being Pagan survivals – Morris dances as fertility rites, say. In the mid C20 Margaret Murray (3) and contemporaries working through the Folklore Society became convinced of the existence of traditional witchcraft, handed down orally through many generations as a survival of the 'Old Religion'. The combination of her ideas and reputation (primarily as an Egyptologist) was a powerful incentive to Gerald Gardiner in his formulation of the modern Pagan religion Wicca in the 1950s – based on eight festivals celebrating the passage of the seasons: Summer and Winter Solstices; Spring & Autumn

Hedingham Fair

CALENDAR OF TRADITIONAL CUSTOMS
2009

The Hedingham Fair Calendar of Traditional Customs 2009 *cover illustrates customs from early spring – clockwise from top left – Burns Night, Valentines Day, Haxey Hood, Candlemas/Imbolc, Hallaton Hare Pie & Bottle Kicking (centre), Olney Pancake Race,*

Equinoxes; Samhain (Halloween); Imbolc (Candlemas); Beltane (May Day) and Lammas (start of August). Unfortunately as Hutton has demonstrated Murray's ideas seemed to have little if any tangible evidence to back them up. Does this mean that in England 'traditional witchcraft' as a survival from pre-Christian belief systems did not exist? It would be difficult to assert this with total confidence although Hutton (4) searched carefully and found no C20 evidence of survivals. This, together with the modern academic fashion for documentary proof perhaps explains why academic approaches to folklore as Pagan survival now run as follows: Britain has been a Christian country for more than a millennium, and where this does not explain folklore phenomena, they are most likely to have derived from popular entertainment (5).

Unfortunately this approach also has significant weaknesses. Folklore does not stop in 1900 – anyone unsure of this should examine the C20 history of Morris Dancing. Although there was no Pagan religion in 1900 (with priests, bureaucracy etc.), there certainly is now, with spiritual and religious significance attached to folk activities by many Pagan people, both participating and watching. Even if folklore could be stopped in 1900, there is any number of recovered customs, stories, plays, songs etc. that neither Christianity nor secularism can explain fully. While they almost certainly do not have pre-Christian origins when viewed in their entirety, parts of them fall outside Christian ideology. The idea of unrecorded transmission through generations thus cannot be discounted, particularly where the passage of the year is being celebrated (ploughing, birth of lambs, spring, May as the coming of summer, Harvest, the coming of winter, the turn of the year). Proving how survivals occurred away from the gaze of Manor and Parsonage is almost impossibly difficult, as one of the essential characteristics of folklore is its orality; much that has survived will have little or no written provenance. However, evidence of 'wise' people living within villages certainly does exist; concentrations of knowledge (herbalism, healing, midwifery, laying out the dead, perhaps forms of divination) existed as an alternative culture and social necessity. There is also reason to believe that village wise women took opportunities to share ideas when they met, and that some with reputations as 'cunning men' were avid book collectors, regularly interacting with urban culture. Some of the songs and tunes in this collection celebrate the passage of the seasons in an old fashioned way, comfortable in the certainty that established Christianity and contemporary secularism cannot deny presence of other popular belief systems either past or present, and free to write songs from more than one spiritual perspective.

The Green Man

Much of this thinking goes back to one morning early in 1998 when Karen woke up with an image (actually two) buzzing around in her consciousness. I was to learn that day to stay quiet when this happened until the idea was fully down on paper – almost always it was worthwhile and productive. This day, it was staggering. Before lunch she had produced two designs, one of a pair of clogs, the other a complex circular Green Man face. Until that time we had not considered specialising in mystical imagery or having much to do with belief systems at all, but the response to this design was instantaneous and it pointed a new direction and a second group of enthusiasts (Pagans) for whom we might be able to develop designs. The Green Man Face (so we called it) remains one of our top selling designs as greetings card, T-shirt, Calendar and book illustration and engraved glass goblet. More than this, it has led both of us to look at vernacular culture in a different way.

This image and the response to it also opened up the idea that there was much more to Folk culture than music – that folk culture is bound up with the history and evolution of the British people themselves from their earliest post ice age beginnings, through the various migrations that had brought Celts, Saxons and Scandinavians to our shores and the alien aristocratic impositions of Rome and Normandy. It opened up the reality that folk customs evolved through the pattern of life itself – planting and sowing, the coming of summer, high summer, the harvests of grain, fruit and meat, the coming of winter and the turn of the year. In course of time this had come to be overlaid by the specific celebrations of individual communities and by the Christian calendar (the year of celebration is dominated by two great cycles of events – one short cycle from just before Christmas until Old Twelfth Night (Jan 17th) and a much longer Easter cycle from Shrove Tuesday until Corpus Christi, a period of about four months when many celebration dates move, synchronised with Easter. We came to believe that certain archetypes seemed to be able to survive whatever religion held sway (the foliate head Green Man as a male archetype and the Triple Hare as a female archetype as two examples of these). Whether or not folk customs were attached to any religion was often a matter of time and circumstance, but the people and the land were cunning, able to carry out religious observance to satisfy authority and then get on with their lives away from the gaze of the Manor or Parsonage. Customs, music, songs, plays evolved with changes in population, living and working conditions, fashion, technology, location of political and / or religious power. Certain things however seemed to remain constant – change itself, the desire of individuals to be creative, the existence of a pattern of linkages between creativity, the mass media of whatever period, publication and transmission / dissemination of ideas, songs, dances etc and their incorporation into the collective and individual memories of the community, including addition to an already existing orally transmitted repertoire.

When I was young Ewan MacColl picked up on this brilliantly, using the relatively new media of radio and recording, and the tried and tested medium of print. As a

Hunting the Earl of Rone, Coombe Martin, N Devon 1999
l to r Chris Mewse, Colin, Karen Cater

The Earl is shot by the Grenadiers, then brought back to life by the actions of the Oss and Teaser

consequence, many modern publications now list 'Dirty Old Town', 'Shoals of Herring', 'Free Born Man' and others he wrote as 'traditional' songs. The same MacColl is frequently dissed as a singer songwriter, purveyor of a product different from and inferior to the 'real' tradition. It isn't difficult to spot the contradiction. As far as Karen and I are concerned, the more we enquired into folk culture and the more broadly we cast our net away from music, the more we saw common processes linking folk experience across centuries – although the media might change, the methods used by MacColl differed little from those used by creatives and publishers ever since the invention of the printing press and probably before that. Now it would be nice to say that this reasoning process was complete before I wrote any songs or tunes – not so, it's a post hoc rationalisation that I'm still working through.

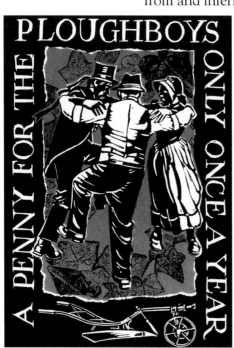

The image that inspired the song – Old Glory Molly Dancers
l to r – John Barnes, Paul Aldis, Ken May

After the warm response to the 'Penny for the Ploughboys' design, I started to wonder if there might be a song in there somewhere. It was to be a long gestation. About a year later the chorus came, driving up to Suffolk one day, but it was to be another couple of years, during part of my sentence to 'supply teaching with hard labour', with the Sixth Form working away diligently on their business studies assignments, that the verses of Penny for the Ploughboys finally emerged. Judging by what has happened since, the wait was worthwhile. The Molly teams took to it instantly. Pete Coe did me the great honour of recording it and taking it all round the country. Several more years passed before the song 'Wassail' happened, gazing out across the North York Moors in high summer, and then 'The Merry Actors' the following winter, by which time I'd realised that I'd taken to writing songs and tunes in the old styles, the styles that the old country people had been steeped in and which the collectors had taken up. Not wishing to be dismissed as a singer songwriter, I thought I'd better start to assemble my retaliation, to be able to get it in first. It didn't take long to realise that there was a substantial windmill at which to tilt.

Re-examining the basis of English Folk Tradition

The search to understand human behaviour stretches across many academic disciplines from history, archaeology and anthropology to politics, psychology and sociology. How behaviour has come to be evaluated in C20 / C21 within organisations or human activities or whole societies has frequently varied according to their size, or technology or communication mechanisms at their disposal, levels of education and literacy, political structures, religion and a whole host of other factors. Interpretation of these factors is as likely to be influenced by the beliefs (perspective) of the evaluator as by any research evidence s/he is sifting through. Strangely, folk music or traditional music has been largely insulated from these processes, though it has never lacked strongly held theories often based on the raw observation, of sometimes very luminous individuals (Sharp, Vaughan Williams, MacColl etc.).

Over the years I have become increasingly convinced that notions of folk 'tradition' need to be re-examined – what England / Britain has is not only a magnificent folk heritage or legacy of song and dance, but several centuries of continuous development, dynamic and constantly adapting to changes in circumstance. Of the early writers on folk music, only William Chappell, himself a music publisher, saw nineteenth century English Popular (folk) Music as part of a continuum stretching back centuries and subject to constant change – although his work concentrated on published music rather than the now much more fashionable orally collected repertoire. There is also evidence to suggest that this process of adaptation continued beyond 1914, after the era of the great collections, particularly through the incorporation of Music Hall songs and songs from the radio into field singers' repertoire. In recent times, particularly since the advent of rock 'n' roll, styles of music in the repertoire of ordinary people may have changed further to be almost unrecognisable from the early C20 collections. Unfortunately, there is little means of knowing this as many folk collectors since 1914 have looked primarily for styles of material that would have survived from pre-1914 times. Modern (i.e. post 1950) collecting, with one or two notable exceptions, has used the pre 1914 template to predetermine what should or should not be classified as 'folk'. Perhaps it is time for musical anthropologists to again become active amongst the English people, without any preconceptions as to what they might look for.

Looking back from the perspective of social history, the three centuries or more prior to industrialisation might be viewed as being 'all of a piece' – with the village for most people the basic unit of social organisation, with only gradual changes in land tenure, farming technology and population. As such it sustained a fairly stable social and musical culture, interacting with the towns as will be shown, despite occasional upheavals, in particular the religious tumult of C16 & 17. Musical fashion came and went, some instruments have either disappeared completely or nearly so: pipes (except in Northumbria); hurdy-gurdy; pipe and tabor. From the middle of C18 onwards though this began to alter – the pace of change picked up in an ever increasing helter-skelter with industrialisation, changes in transport, radio & TV and the internet, to name but a few developments.

For a long time it was believed that England had no National musical culture (Sharp – 'Some Conclusions' reporting Carl Engel). When a very rich musical heritage was uncovered it was apparent that the social conditions which had generated it were evaporating, giving rise to the claim that folk music would die out unless urgent steps were taken to recover it. Arguably this takes a very narrow view of English vernacular musical heritage. Collectors were unashamedly selective, not only editing out anything they could identify as contemporary, but also disregarding vernacular music preserved in printed form and old style religious songs and music persisting in the countryside. In short, they were an interest group with a variety of agendas. What they recovered was the snapshot of English people's culture they wanted to see, not the total picture.

Cecil Sharp and the Great Collections

The term 'folk' first emerged in C19 Europe, principally to identify stories and music drawn from 'the people', different from those circulating in polite society, but capable of being harnessed for social improvement (through fairy tales or orchestral music) in a rapidly changing world. From the middle of C19 up to 1914 and beyond, British awareness of 'folk' led to increasing attempts to recover songs, dances, plays, lore that circulated in the countryside and seemed in danger of being superseded by changes in social structure and popular fashion. Learned societies were established: the Folklore Society (1878); Folk Song Society (1898) and English Folk Dance Society (1911) to research, recover and publish information about the nature and practice of quite detailed aspects of vernacular culture, customs and traditions. From the outset, these bodies tended towards an Arcadian standpoint, harking back to an idealised Merry England, before industrialisation and enclosure, which probably never quite existed. Much of the thinking was also internationalist, drawing comparisons between English vernacular culture and more 'primitive' cultures in Europe and the British Empire. Customs and ceremonies that didn't fall within Anglican experience were lumped together as 'Pagan', airbrushing out centuries of history and assuming that all belief systems were supported by enormous bureaucracies as was the case with the British churches.

Pre-eminent amongst English folklorists was Cecil Sharp whose Herculean labours of collection and dissemination in the fields of folk song and dance fully deserve the accolade 'great'. However, preservation was the spirit of the age and little thought was given to how the folk repertoire might have come into being. Collectors reported that England had been a 'nest of singing birds'(6) until about 1860 when mysteriously the people's repertoire failed to transfer to the upcoming generation, so that by 1900 it seemed in danger of dying out with the older people. The collectors gave little thought to the possible effects of C19 social changes on the people's song repertoire. In less than a century after 1800 the English population had increased fourfold. Cramped, squalid industrial towns and warren like factories had replaced open fields as the locus of existence for many. The nature of village life was also being changed by a combination of enclosure and technological change. Railways and the popular press shortened communication times creating countryisation (a sort of C19 globalisation). It could have been considered that musical experience might possibly have adjusted with changes in the pace of life, and that the urban Music Halls were as much a reflection of restructured society as they were an innovation. Instead, it became generally accepted that the musical harvest of the countryside was magnificent and that it was superior to the urban popular music of the day. However, with the right approach it could be reprogrammed and recirculated as an agent to foster both national identity and social improvement.

The great collector

To demonstrate the purity of vernacular tradition, Sharp et al adopted the notion of 'the peasant' as a sociological ideal type, similar to the concept of 'the folk' already circulating academically. These were people devoid of industrial taint in whom the real spirit of England resided. They were stolid country people, almost all unlettered labourers, whose music had been handed down for generations through villages and families, substantially different from contemporary popular culture. However, they were in the main advancing in years and many had not sung regularly since their youth. It was never admitted that these so called 'peasants' might themselves have acquired their songs from a variety of sources: including books of ancient ballads; penny broadside sheets, Chapbooks and Garlands of songs circulating constantly in both countryside and towns; theatrical sources including ballad operas, ballad booths – a regular feature of many country fairs, local professional singers and even the early C19 Music Hall itself. It now seems likely that any of these sources might be an agent producing song variations; and that they were received by country people, who were a good deal more curious than given credit for, and constantly selected what they liked best, rejecting the rest to create many of the characteristics of oral tradition. Where unusual oral phenomena were reported, identifying their specialness far outweighed any attempt to understand how this had come to be. Many country songs had 'modal' melodies – a musical form thought to have vanished several centuries earlier. As it was mistakenly assumed that all country music and song was secular, the possible link between modality and psalm singing in popular religion was missed. Neither was a possible modal connection between the travelling gypsy community and the musical experience of their host communities fully explored.

In the course of the next few pages, I hope to set out some of the ways in which popular sources might have fed into country singing (and later, dance as well). The reader should also assume a melting pot with constant overlap rather than a structure with rigid demarcation lines.

The Antiquarian Ballad Editors

At regular intervals from the time of the Restoration of the Monarchy (1660) for at least two centuries, articulate antiquarian literary editors published bound books of ancient poetry and / or ballads. Most of these were obtained from either printed or manuscript sources, with only a very small amount recovered orally. As Harker's 'Fakesong', written from a Marxian standpoint, argues these antiquarian editors were nearly all 'mediators'(7), with no real identification with or feeling for working people, but prepared to change the words of ballads to support their own social agendas. Some were not above substantial text rewriting; Bishop Percy ('Reliques of Ancient English Poetry', 1765) was eventually unmasked as a substantial faker in the 1860s. Theoretical arguments about the nature of ballads abounded, often from contradictory viewpoints. Ballad origins were unclear. Perhaps there had been generations of travelling minstrels, many of them gypsies. Perhaps ballad origins were oral, predating the printing press. For many editors the 'best' ballads were deemed to have an impersonal quality to them, with rough edges removed by contact with a large number of people over an extended time period. Conversely, by almost common consent ballads were likely to be tainted by contemporary changes, particularly contact with the 'broadside' press or 'common' people or peasantry – folk music tainted by 'the folk'! Some editors were clearly aware they were publishing songs, for others ancient poetry was to be recited in the drawing rooms of the well to do. Some editors benefited from private patronage; others from involvement with learned societies which seemed to flourish in England until around 1850. A few published their works commercially, i.e. they needed to sell in significant quantities to make sufficient money to provide them with a living. Most eventually fed into the melting pot which would produce F. J. Child's English and Scottish Popular Ballads.

The paradox of Harker's argument lies in his assertion that the ballad editors were divorced from the ordinary working people. In saying this he unwittingly asserts, both that the social basis of English popular / folk song is broader than just 'the folk', and that the book collections played a significant (in some cases interactive) part in its development. Among the mediators he lists are Bruce and Stokoe, who's 'Northumbrian Minstrelsy' (1882) did play a significant role in shaping the musical identity of the North Eastern region, both inside folk music and generally. A similar claim can be made for John Harland's Ballads and Songs of Lancashire (1865), reflecting songs in existing popular repertoire and providing a fund for singers to draw on for the future. As for Child, his magnum opus went through three separate editions, all drawn from 'mediated' sources – the first in the 1850s predominately from printed sources; the final one (published gradually between 1882 and 1898) including substantial material from collections assembled from oral sources, particularly the Buchan MSS. What links all these written sources together is that a substantial part of their offering continued to circulate orally amongst people both in the USA and Britain who were very unlikely to have come into contact with antiquarian ballad collections. Right up until the 1960s it remained a folk song collector's ultimate dream to recover a Child Ballad from a field source, even better a Robin Hood Ballad. If folk music is / were ever the music of 'the people', it clearly traversed between the lettered and the unlettered.

Singing Sam of Derby, 18th century ballad seller

The Broadside Press

One possible connection between antiquarian ballad collections and the people might be Broadside printers who from the early C17 were set up in nearly all towns of any size, but particularly in London. Ballad collections in manuscript form pre-date the printing press but from the mid C16, printers had to be licensed by the Stationers Company (8), and broadsides, normally printed on one side only on low quality paper were the province of poorer printers. It is likely that Broadside printers were able to draw on the antiquarian ballad collections as source material. Before 1700 most broadsides were of varying size, set in an old style Gothic type called 'Black Letter', frequently illustrated with woodcuts and set up in two or more columns. Subject matter was frequently political, particularly anticlerical, which may explain much of the ballad popularity of Robin Hood. On December 14th 1624, one hundred and twenty eight ballads were licensed including 'Chevvy Chase', 'Lord Bateman', 'Sir John Barley Corne' and others which subsequently survived and developed for centuries. Neither was it unusual for songs to circulate between ballad printers and the countryside and back again, so that a popular song from a generation past might re-emerge as "A New Ballad upon . . ." This clearly happened to 'The Spotted Cow', 'The Merry Haymakers' and many other songs. Other 'new' ballads were described as being 'set to the tune of . . .', usually a popular melody that would help them both sell and circulate amongst the wider community. Whilst some sections of polite society frowned on Broadside Ballads as vulgar, they were collected in vast numbers by such luminaries as Samuel Pepys and John, Duke of Roxburghe who in 1788 become owner of a Broadside Ballad collection (subsequently known as the 'Roxburghe Ballads') numbering some 1300 items begun some years earlier by Robert Harley, Earl of Oxford.

At the beginning of the C18, the printing style changed with the introduction of 'Whiteletter Balladsheets', which afforded greater flexibility to the printer and a chance to incorporate greater amounts of text. Subject matter changed – many of the songs being those currently popular and reflecting the bawdy style much in vogue – wenches, frolicks, cuckolding, whores – the stuff of D'Urfey's 'Pills to Purge Melancholy'. Sometimes a sheet would be folded once, twice or more times creating a 'Chapbook' (literally a cheap-book). Sometimes a group of songs would be linked together to create a 'Garland', possibly including sermons, stories, jests, almanacks and, as is now known, Mummers Plays. Chapbooks etc would be circulated through the villages by Pedlars, frequently called 'Chapmen', also selling household goods and plying their wares at markets and fairs, circulating news, tunes and entertainment and always having a good ear for what they might pick up. Usually, after they had gone the sheets were pasted up in pubs and other places, so that those who could read could learn them and transmit them more generally among the communities. With the growth of industrialisation, printing became more mechanised and the large scale Broadside printers of the C19 emerged: Catnach and Pitts of Seven Dials, London; Such of Borough Market, London; Harkness of Preston – all independents whose success depended on their ability to sell. A good murder ballad like 'Maria Marten' might sell over two million copies. At least five different versions of 'John Barleycorn' were published by Such between 1840 and 1900. Whilst there can be no doubt that country people honed and refined the broadsides smoothing out many of the irregularities of the often hastily constructed doggerel, the folk song collections of the early C20 bear testament to the success of the Broadside industry – the wide dissemination of some now well known songs probably couldn't have happened without it. It is also probable that Chapmen had a vested interest in variety and novelty – certainly F. J. Child saw a clear relationship between professional singers and songs changing (9).

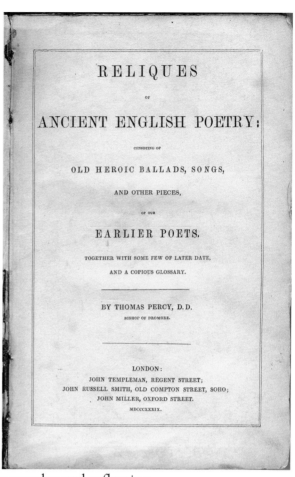

"Percy's Reliques"

Music of the Theatre

According to William Chappell's 'Popular Music of the Olden Time' (10), another likely source of much music found in the countryside is the theatre. 'I cannot eat but little meat' is described by Chappell as the "first drinking song of any merit in our language", and while probably having origins in manuscript was included in the comedy 'Gammer Gurton's Needle', performed in 1575. In modern times we know it as a country song, a Morris Dance tune ('Mrs Casey') and as an Irish polka from Co. Cork. Its actual line of development is unclear but the tune certainly appears in Ritson's 'English Songs' (1783). Jumping forward from 1575, the musical theatre flourished in the C17 spirited and bawdy reaction to the suppression of Puritanism after the Restoration in 1660. Its principal luminary, Tom D'Urfey, friend of Charles II and best known for authoring 'Pills to Purge Melancholy' (1719-20, reprinted 1959) was also a prolific songwriter, whose success owed much to his practice of setting songs to well known ballad airs, and possibly to dance tunes as well. Here, demarcations become difficult. Country Dance music was very much the spirit of the age and a number of publishers used it profitably, particularly Walsh, Wright but above all Playford whose finest work 'The Dancing Master' was published in 1696. Many of these airs were incorporated into countless theatrical productions, alongside ballads and contemporary popular songs; so much so that the John Clare MSS, assembled nearly a century later contain theatrical music, country fiddle and pipe tunes and songs from old ballad sheets, sadly with no tunes noted down (11). Even recognising that wide ranging changes in musical style occurred during the early Tudor period, it seems that English music and song had integrity, which combined with a relatively slow pace of change, ensured that by 1800 it had lasted in largely unbroken tradition for considerably more than two centuries – a tradition that would continue well into the C19. Given the transmission mechanisms from town to country and back again that are now known to have existed, it must be very unlikely that a repertoire entirely separate from that of the broadsheet printers and theatre owners could have been growing up in the countryside.

Ballad sellers would sing their wares in the street to attract attention and encourage passers-by to stop and purchase the latest songs.

In 1727, a near revolutionary change occurred – the staging of the 'Beggars Opera' by John Gay (12). This contained over forty new songs, was received rapturously and its influence extends to this day (in the personae of Dibdin, Gilbert and Sullivan, Novello, Bart, Bellamy, Lloyd Webber and many others both British and American). Among the songs was 'Over the Hills and far Away'. Within a very short time Ballad Operas dominated the London theatres, a situation that would continue for a century, providing an almost unending source of material for the ballad publishers, costermongers, chapmen and pedlars, and an equally certain trickle down into the countryside – that is not to say that all songs from ballad operas survived to be collected as folk songs. In Thakeray's 'Vanity Fair', the mother of heroine Becky Sharp is described as an 'opera singer' – this does not mean some overweight diva singing in Italian – rather someone treading the boards on the London stage in the ballad operas.

By the beginning of C19 however, the wind of change was blowing. Advances had been made in agriculture, iron smelting, harnessing water power and canal transport. Railways, steam powered textile machinery, factories and towns and above all population explosion would soon follow. People in the towns had to be entertained and the entertainment had to be relevant – to resonate with their mode of life. Change was gradual initially – the Music Hall performer Harry Clifton, working in the 1860s wrote and popularised songs like 'Country Carrier', to be collected as a folk song less than forty years later as well as 'Calico Printer's Clerk' taken up by the folk movement a century later. The famed North Eastern artiste, Geordie Ridley, author of 'Blaydon Races' seems to have drawn his inspiration for the verse and the tale from the song 'Settle Fair', originally published as a Broadside by Harkness of Preston, and on the air 'Wensleydale Lad' (13). By the end of C19 this grand and extended period of contiuous development of English vernacular music was all but over. Songs by new stars like Harry Champion, initially rejected by the folk song collectors would eventually find their way into popular repertoire and into the folk movement. In 1860, this new music was revolutionary. By 1900, all was not yet lost. Singers like Lucy White and Louie Hooper and many others would provide Sharp et al with an enormous treasury of songs. But then wasn't their mother Mrs England, a very well known local professional ballad singer?

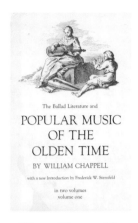

Wm. Chappell's "Popular Music of the Olden Time"

Unbroken Tradition – a Process of Transformation

At this point it might be worthwhile to reintroduce some possible means of evaluating tradition briefly mentioned earlier: is folk heritage the music of the countryside or of the whole community? should oral tradition as communicated to collectors continue to be valued as pre-eminent or should greater value be placed on printed sources? how significant is continuousness in tradition? is folk transmission of greater value when located within individual families or communities? is folk expression the milieu solely of working class people or of the whole community?

Anyone seeking to evaluate tradition on the basis of the broad sweep of English vernacular music from both oral and printed sources is likely to be confronted with a conundrum – the singularity of oral tradition as recovered at the beginning of C20 and the extent to which it differs from music handed down through written sources. Nowhere do C17 – C19 mass communication media begin to explain the survival of modal forms of musical expression thought to have been long extinct in the countryside. Because Broadsides did not include tunes, there is little evidence that might shed light on how tune variants developed, and the varying degrees of importance of chapmen and country singers in this process. It is very possible to see why Sharp etc argued for the untainted musical purity of informants.

However, it seems equally clear that written sources, mainly Broadside and theatrical, did regularly interact with the traditions of the countryside, both reinforcing them and adding to them. It seems that the special skill of country people and of several centuries of uninterrupted socio cultural development was to

Mummers Plays were often seen as part of the Christmas festivities

Handsworth Longsword danced on Boxing Day

effect processes of transformation; including retaining the beauties of the modal song structures and applying them to new songs as they filtered down; regularly précising the lugubrious doggerel of the Broadsides to create shorter more incisive songs; and generating many of the tune variants. Similar processes seem to have occurred with both country dance and generation of village Morris Dance and Sword Dance traditions; with adaptation of Mummers Plays and with constant changes to Christmas festivities handed down as Wassailing. In reality a much broader social consensus including the towns was involved in the making of country songs etc so that they can truly be identified as part of national musical culture, with obvious regional and local variations. It is a matter of the history of folklore that the contribution of lettered people seems to have been considerably undervalued in comparison with the unlettered; similarly middle class people when compared with the working classes. In the future, without diminishing oral tradition, it is arguable that printed sources need to be accorded higher value.

In the past folk transmission has often been modelled as a linear process, possibly involving gradual atrophy with age and failing memory, or across generations. As an alternative, and in the light of arguments above, it may be more realistic to propose a circular and continuous process model, called here the 'Variant Transformation Model'. On this basis recovery of oral material by collectors might be directly equated with creation / writing of new material, with both feeding into processes of dissemination – whether by the books, broadsides, chapmen and fairs of centuries past or the live performances, books, radio / TV, recordings of modern times, any of which media might provide a source from which people can learn songs. In this way the much criticised part of the work of Cecil Sharp in rewriting songs and publishing them for schools, and his formation of EFDS in 1911 can be seen as 'all of a piece' with his collecting. It is almost inconceivable that a C21 Sharp would not have used every mass medium at his disposal to return the culture of the English people to the English people, irrespective of what he might have thought of music played in nightclubs, stadiums and open air festivals.

However, for many folklorists, songs and dances must undergo processes of change and transformation, away from contact with mass media, in order to become 'folk', different from their original form. It is clear that folk process as change existed in the countryside probably for several centuries, but that change was gradual. It is possible to chart the decline of the great narrative ballads in Broadside collections as C17 passed into C18 & C19, but they did not disappear from country singers' repertoires overnight. There may be reason to speculate about the extent to which variant changes took place consciously or subconsciously – behavioural literature abounds with descriptions of and theories about 'change agents', and many suggest themselves in the folk arena – printers, chapmen, competitions such as those held as part of Dover's Games; aristocratic patrons of local customs such as the Bagot family at Abbots Bromley, Staffordshire, the collectors themselves. However processes of transformation complete this circular model, enabling folk process to be conceptualised as involving (a) collection / recovery and new creation; (b) dissemination; (c) learning and activity (d) transformation leading back to collection and recovery.

In the past folk transmission has often been modelled as a linear process. It may be more realistic to propose a circular and continuous process model where processes of aesthetic transformation complete the cycle

VARIANT TRANSFORMATION MODEL
FOR PRE MUSIC HALL VERNACULAR CULTURE

Learning
Participation & Activity

Dissemination through all
media available in the period

Change &Transformation
often over a long period

Collection & Recovery
Creation of new material

Impact of the Music Halls

If this model does provide a basis on which to evaluate the unbroken tradition of several centuries, it is not clear that it is useful in explaining changes to musical culture since the mid C19. Nearly all folk song collectors report the failure of the old traditions to pass to the upcoming generations from the mid C19. Whilst being aware of the dangers of circular argument, members of the post 1945 'baby boom' generation have lived through the rock 'n' roll musical revolution. Half a century later, the old pre-rock music survives, on Radio 2, in seaside shows, classic record reissues and elsewhere. It is plausible to draw some parallel with the C19. As social conditions changed, particularly urbanisation, factory work, railway transport and seaside holidays, so modes of entertainment also began to shift. This appears also to have been a gradual process, but with a definite tipping point, although Kidson (1891) reports Broadsides, even of great ballads like 'Lord Bateman' continuing to circulate until just before his publication date (14). Kidson's notes make it clear that he collected both from oral sources, many of whom were lettered, as

Chelmsford Folk Club Mummers play 1971
l to r – Roger Johnson, & Colin Cater as 'Basher' & 'Slasher'; play written by Geoff Harris

well as being able to retrace the development of songs back to Broadsides and into the antiquarian collections, which continued well into C19 (Halliwell, 1841; Dixon, 1857; Logan, 1869; Bruce & Stokoe, 1882). However with the population explosion came a printing explosion and vast expansion in the numbers of titles offered, often just tracts without any musical content, though Garrett reckons that as late as 1861, there were over 700 ballad singers plying their trade in London alone (15).

In the mid C19 other changes occurred: newspapers sprung up in nearly all large towns with London titles often circulating nationally; magazines, notably Punch and Illustrated London News emerged. Form the 1840s Music Halls began to evolve out of the London cyder cellars, coffee houses and salons, bringing named artistes to the fore. Many of these doubled as music publishers; separate from the broadsheet printers, but by the 1850s both purpose built Halls such as the Canterbury Tavern in Pimlico and music publishing companies began to develop. It was a short step to 'star' singers such as Sam Cowell, Harry Clifton, Gus Elen, Harry Champion, Vesta Tilley, Marie Lloyd and many others. It was an equally short step to sheet music and hit songs such as 'Ratcatchers Daughter', 'Polly Perkins', 'Oh Mr Porter', 'Any Old Iron' and thousands of others. Once established, the Music Hall spread all over the country like a bush fire. As successive copyright acts gradually strengthened the law to include musical performance, so the concept of ownership of music and performance grew. The former situation of town produced song being transformed in the countryside began to give way to something more structured. It is not difficult to see how people were dazzled by the new entertainment medium: equally why the literati and musicians of the Folk Song Society were appalled by it.

Fred Smy singing in the Middleton Bell, Suffolk, where regular sessions of music, song & step dancing still happen in the 21st century

Of course, the Music Hall repertoire did pass into the countryside – Sharp et al were quite candid about their selectivity in not noting it down from their singer informants, though as the presence of songs like 'Buttercup Joe', 'Down in the Fields', 'Country Carrier' and others indicate, they couldn't always spot the difference. The old music was also a long time declining, and as later collections like 'Songs Sung in Suffolk' (16) indicate the old repertoire and the new gradually melded together. However, folk process transformation all but disappeared at a stroke. How many country variants of Music Hall Songs like 'Ratcatcher's Daughter' or 'Polly Perkins' (disregarding 'Cushie Butterfield', which like 'Polly Perkins' is an urban Music Hall song) have ever been noted down? One or two Music Hall songs, particularly when generated away from London do appear to have produced regional variants and maybe textual and melodic ones as well. 'Mrs Merry's Ball' springs to mind. But they were much fewer in number than in former times.

More than anything this reflects changes in social organisation. Rather than being the sum of constituent parts, united by language and culture but politically disparate, England was becoming centralised with the pace of life increasing – the way in which railway lines converge on London and then stop illustrates this as does the pre-eminence of London newspapers (and later the BBC) over their regional and local counterparts. Sheet music and copyright brought ownership of music. A new hit song could travel the country in weeks if not days whereas broadside and chapbook sellers would have taken much longer. When radio and recording came this was reinforced, so that there was often just not time for the old slow transforming processes to work. Once a new song was published, there was always a strong likelihood that it would become set in stone – a process which continued (in many cases) when the old repertoire started to be re-popularised with the growth of the folk song clubs. Mass education brought greater literacy, again arguably an obstacle to change, also something that would quickly reduce the supply of unlettered country singers to a trickle. By the time that 'English Folk Song – Some Conclusions' was published, the world it described had already passed beyond recapture. If 'the folk' ever had existed their day was done. Of those who survived many were slaughtered on the Western Front. Even the Copper Family – singers in linear family tradition over seven generations whose songs vary in antiquity between early C18 and early C20, and who for many are the very essence of English Traditional singing, acquired their repertoire by a centralising process, codifying their songs into a family song book in the 1930s (17), since when scarcely another has been added. The Coppers possess a folk provenance almost unequalled, yet there is little evidence of old style transformation about them in the last fifty years. Clearly the world had changed.

The Copper Family at Essex Singers Club June 1996
l to r –
John Copper, Bob Copper, Jill & John Dudley, (Karen Cater far right)

Folk Music in Modern Times – Developments in Dance

Formation of the Folk Song Society (1898) is thought by many to have inaugurated the folk music movement in Britain. Very few historical eras are able to be separated absolutely from what preceded them and so it is in this case. Collection was already under way (inc. the Broadwoods, Baring Gould and Kidson): the Folklore Society was already two decades old. With the arrival of Sharp and Mary Neal, dance was brought within the folk fold. In C20, large scale popular interest in folk dance, both social and ceremonial, predates popular interest in song. Formation of the English Folk Dance Society (1911) generated a national network of local and county based organisations, able to come together on occasion to stage a National festival – possibly for the first time the locus of folk activity had shifted from the village / locality to the club / interest, a pattern that would grow as C20 unfolded. In 1922, the 'Travelling Morrice', all Cambridge alumni, was formed, touring all over England but particularly in the Cotswolds, and eventually giving rise to the formation of the Morris Ring, again using the club model, in 1934. Inspired by Sharp's labours, leading figures were keen to collect, preserve, disseminate and perform everything they perceived as having come from 'the tradition'.

After Sharp's death, EFDS under Douglas Kennedy (EFDSS after amalgamation with the Folk Song Society in 1932) was keen to modernise social dance in line with a populist folk dance movement developing in the USA, eventually to become post war square dance boom, enjoying even Royal enthusiasm in the early 1950s. Between 1947 and 1964 the Community Dance Manuals (18) were published in seven volumes providing a core repertoire for a generation of bands and dancers. Unfortunately this also skewed the movement opening it up to overt

Beaux of London City, dancing 'The Rose', formed by Peter Kennedy in 1947 as a touring demonstration team

Chelmsford Morris, formed 1972
Music: l to r – Jennie Davis, Carole Cottrill, Colin, Gary Davis

American influences, until largely reversed by a strong reaction beginning in the 1970s. Extensive use of workshops, books, recordings and internet has been made throughout, although social dance has existed largely outside the gaze of the mass media, allowing many of the more fluid aspects of folk transformation processes to operate.

Thanks largely to the popular boom coming from the folk song clubs in the 1970s, Morris Dancing has enjoyed a golden age during the last three decades. Without interfering with those villages whose performance traditions were largely unbroken from C19, Morris (initially Cotswold Morris) had spread all over the country, as people sought to rediscover the lost traditions of England (this also fuelled interest in Mumming, Wassailing and many annual customs). Although somewhat blighted by gender bigotry during the 1960s and 70s, many dancers increasingly looked outwards from Cotswold Morris either towards the dance traditions of their own locality or for a louder more energetic experience. Folk festival workshops offered Border Morris, North West Morris, Step Clog, Molly Dancing, Appalachian, Fluffy Morris and inspired by Shropshire Bedlams, Seven Champions, Garstang, Gloucestershire Old Spot, Windsor Morris, Trefor Owen and many more, teams sprang up all over the country. The gender problem was neatly sidestepped by formation of (Women's) Morris Federation and Open Morris leaving the Morris Ring in a sort of misogynistic limbo from which hopefully they will eventually be able to extricate themselves. All Morris clubs regularly come together in Days of Dance. Repertoire has expanded exponentially; even some Ring sides make their own dances up. The recovered Cotswold repertoire has been published in full (19) providing a still largely untapped resource. With Border and Molly repertoire less sustained by publications to standardise things, new dances have mushroomed, spreading orally, making Morris dancing of all folk activities in modern times one that conforms well to a transformation model of tradition.

Persephone from Bradford, Yorkshire, dance North-West clog Morris

Folk song clubs, the folk boom and then . . .

Starting in 1953 the Ballads and Blues Club meeting at the Princess Louise in High Holborn probably counts as the first folk song club, numbering Bert Lloyd, Ewan MacColl, Isla Cameron, Seamus Ennis and Alan Lomax amongst its residents, and initially with no clear policy on what should be or should not be sung (20). Traditional songs whether from field singers or printed sources rubbed shoulders with 'Sixteen Tons'. When Peggy Seeger arrived in the UK in 1956, she and MacColl, with Charles Parker embarked on the Radio Ballad projects which involved recording actual speech often from field singers such as Sam Larner of Winterton, Norfolk and members of the Stewart family of Blairgowrie Scotland. From this came drama, stories and many of MacColl's best songs. Eventually, Ballads and Blues introduced a policy pushing people to sing in the voice and accent in which they spoke. Soon afterwards, in 1960, it was reorganised to become the 'Singers Club'. At this stage, few people questioned the existence of newly written material alongside folk songs from times past. In his autobiography, MacColl recounts how the great Norfolk field singer Harry Cox had learned the ballad Van Dieman's Land from a ballad sheet and set the tune himself. He might have made up some words too if he had been able to write them down. Nobody questioned that singers introduced variations into their tunes to help them interpret words – it was accepted as a natural part of the singers' art. Neither were leading performers like Peggy Seeger and Bert Lloyd above altering songs to make them fit current circumstances – this was after all what broadside printers and chapmen had been doing for centuries.

The demise of the Broadside press (this with many apologies to John Foreman who has continued printing until the present time) clearly had not brought an end to song making in the old Ballad styles, as the songs of Tommy Armstrong and many other industrial workers over the next century demonstrate. In 'Come all Ye Bold Miners' (21), Bert Lloyd presents an impressive industrial Garland, drawing on antiquarian, theatrical and broadside sources as well as contemporary writers such as Ed Pickford and Johnny Handle. There is some evidence of song variant transformation ('Blantyre Explosion', 'Trimdon Grange' and possibly 'Gresford Disaster') but it is limited. The success of the folk movement generated an outpouring of contemporary writing in the old styles: Cyril Tawney wrote about life on the submarines; Graham Miles, Ron Angel and Vin Garbutt wrote about the industrial culture of Teesside; Roger Watson about North Nottinghamshire; John Connolly about Grimsby and the fishing; Ralph MacTell about the 'Streets of London', and there were many, many others. It seemed that creativity, work and celebrating locality were linked inextricably in a modern forward looking movement. There also seemed no reason why this should not spread culturally as Nic Jones' new tunes and settings for old songs and Peter Bellamy's settings to Kipling poems and wonderful Ballad Opera 'The Transports' showed.

Music & creativity, a marriage of ideas – artwork for their wedding invitation. Karen & Colin Cater 1995

So what happened? How did this vibrant and creative song movement run out of puff? Well, like Topsy it grew but like any healthy phenomenon full of intelligent people, it splintered as people developed their own specialisms. Somehow the Ballads and Blues policy of singing in your own voice transmuted folkloristically into notions of anti-Americanism, into opposition to singing with instrumental accompaniment and into a traditional / contemporary divide. Use of the guitar became a major bone of contention – for many it became the very antithesis of English tradition. Parts of the folk movement continued to look forward and outward, particularly Ashley Hutchings, Steeleye Span, Pentangle and Fairport Convention, all of whom were keen to harness folk tradition to contemporary musical sounds, and with considerable success, including getting into 'the charts'. On the other hand some of the more successful club performers were forced to turn completely towards mainstream entertainment as the only feasible means of making a living and were lost to the folk movement (these included Billy Connolly, Gerry Rafferty, Toni Arthur and Jasper Carrot).

For others in the movement, the preferred directions of gaze were backwards and inwards. There were suddenly myriad ways of defining what was 'traditional' and more significantly what was 'not traditional'. Many of these harked back to Sharp – unaccompanied singing; transmission in families again as an ideal, without any recognition of changing times; real traditional singers had to have had the good fortune to be born in the countryside. Other approaches tended to be more (working) class based; only people who subscribed to the Marxian dream were acceptable. However, a great deal boiled down to what a relatively small number of key individuals personally liked or did not like. Often these individuals acted as gatekeepers to the whole movement, in the process establishing a form of folk 'political correctness' guarded by a shadowy 'thought police' – the movement had become prey to a form of snobbery.

Not all effects of turning inwards have been negative. Out of the folk club movement came a network of Folk Festivals, spanning the whole year and the entire country, creating an industry with a recently estimated annual value of £70 million. Sound recording has replaced the Broadside press as the main engine of song renewal and change: any number of companies, many of them run privately by singers themselves, has been set up with some offering an extensive catalogue; an ever increasing number of songs has been recorded and re-recorded, with individual singers' variations to and reconstructions of both words and tunes. After a splurge of book publishing in the 1950s and 1960s, and with the splendid exception of Roy Palmer – a one man industry – publication of new song books tailed off, a process now happily reversed. As with recordings, books have also offered opportunities for songs to be reconstructed or rewritten (22). Sea song and shanty singing which had narrowed down to one or two traditional adherents, Stan Hugill and Bob Roberts, has enjoyed a glorious renaissance, leading to its own circuit of Festivals. The baroque style country music derived from recovered manuscript collections from C18 / C19 and the religious songs of the West Galleries have enjoyed an equally Phoenician rise after a very long sleep.

In the early folk song movement singers rushed to the guitar in droves, without thinking that this instrument had not been available to earlier generations. For others the guitar was anathema because it had not existed in times past and thus could not be described as 'traditional'. Some even put about the fiction that English traditional singing was and always had been 'solo unaccompanied' More than this, certain guitar playing styles (particularly strumming) had an obviously damaging effect on both melodies and lyrics in the 'folk' repertoire. In 'Folk Song in England', pp 66 – 68 (23), Bert Lloyd uses a Romanian example to demonstrate changes in style and atmosphere of vernacular music in a pre-industrial setting. Between 1913, when Bartok visited and a subsequent visit in 1953, the music was greatly altered, attributed by Lloyd to changes in the environmental situation of the singers. Although instrumental accompaniment is not mentioned specifically, there is a clear implication that singers used what was available to them. Using a combination of hindsight and this logic, the ideological proscription of the guitar

Guitars weren't always anathama!

by parts of the folk movement in the 1960s and 1970s, justified by a backwards looking concept of 'authenticity', seems an act of ignorant vandalism.

As a consequence, many guitarists, and those with more interest in contemporary events including their own situations, turned away from the folk movement either towards rock 'n' roll or alternatively made their own contemporary scene. In the process contact was lost with the incoming stream of young people who had seen folk grow in the 1960s and 1970s. More than this by the mid 1980s, for the first time for three decades, most of the contact between folk and mainstream popular music had withered almost to nothing – making folk a musical genre running only in parallel to the mainstream, as it had been in the first half of C20.

Approaches to 'Tradition' in the Modern World

During C20 / C21, despite worst predictions, English vernacular culture has survived and grown, not just the singing and dance repertoire of the great folk collections but across the broader picture of English popular music as identified by Chappell. During the last decade or so, the dance tune repertoire of the eighteenth century has been gradually rediscovered, often in private manuscript books sometimes also containing religious music. The same has been true of the religious song repertoire sung in the West Galleries. Despite being recovered from the printed page, both of these are as English and as much of a 'folk' product as anything recovered orally by the collectors. Together with revivals of folk carols particularly in South Yorkshire / North Midlands, to say nothing of many revived customs this suggests that vernacular traditions can flourish again sometimes after a very long time gap. It simply doesn't matter if there is a major interruption in transmission. As an example can it be said that the Morris Dances of Fieldtown (where there was an interruption of decades between the village team stopping and the dances being taken up in an urban environment) are any less traditional than those of Bampton where there has been no break. There may be differences in performance style giving rise to a possible hierarchy of value, but that is not a matter of traditionality, it is style.

Survival through C20 has required adaptation to changing social conditions. The slow pace of life generating oral transmission has mainly disappeared; the social basis of tradition carriers has changed; modes of communication and recording similarly. Effects of these changes have not been uniform: some folk environments have become more centralised while others, particularly some of the Morris styles, remain diffused. Performance styles have been influenced by the increasing availability of (relatively) cheap instruments. Replacement of the pipe and tabor with the fiddle, then free reed instruments is not regarded as exceptionable anywhere in the Morris world – it's just progress. Perhaps the concertina boom came too late for the early collectors' informants, though Kimber played the Anglo Concertina for Headington Morris in 1899 (and Sharp is reputed to have purchased an English Concertina for the singer Mrs Hooper). In matters of instrumental accompaniment, dancers have tended to make use of whatever is available to them, often with sizeable Morris bands, sometimes electronically amplified.

For many folk song enthusiasts, coming to terms with instruments and accompaniment has been a much more tortuous process. Songs sung in styles predicted as going extinct by Sharp et al continued to be recovered throughout C20 as a smattering of country singers (some with large repertoires) provided repertoire for collectors like Morean, Peter Kennedy, Graney, Hamer, Stubbs, MacColl and Seeger, Henderson, Summers, Howson and others, particularly in Scotland and East Anglia, possibly because of the slower pace of rural lifestyle. Inflow of migrants, particularly Irish and Romany may also have contributed. In addition a substantial tune hoard has been recovered, particularly from East Anglia and Northumbria and an equally substantial collection of folk plays, from almost everywhere in England except East Anglia. There is clear evidence of fresh input into the country singers' repertoire particularly from the radio, but this does not seem to have had time to generate the variant transformations common in times past. However, this raises the issue that if Music Hall songs can be added to traditional song repertoire, as some collectors appear to have done, why not skiffle or rock 'n' roll? There are after all a lot of old boys out there playing it in pubs who haven't been near the media for decades.

For some folk people, tradition has become more a matter of performance style (e.g. solo unaccompanied singing) than of song transformation, with several different styles pre-eminent in different locations within the movement. Others contend that what is really important is location – where the music comes from or from whom – this argument is often used where songs can be traced to families, or villages / communities, or working class people, or country areas. Lineage from any one of these sources would generate hierarchy of value. A third indicator of tradition for many is repertoire, with the orally collected hoard pre-eminent over printed sources. Fourthly, attitudes to creativity as part of folk tradition have varied; with some striving to ensure that the heritage looks outward and forward engaging with the wider community particularly the young, while others look back towards the countryside.

So how should 'tradition' be evaluated in the early years of C21? It seems that the transformation model of previous times is no longer universally applicable. Songs, tunes and dances increasingly pass into the repertoire of ordinary people in a form largely unchanged from how they were created. Existence of sound recordings and their constant reissue as technology becomes updated may also make creative transformation difficult, unless this is done consciously. However, many people continue to sing and play well away from media spotlight in the increasingly informal arena of 'sessions' and 'round the room' singarounds.

'Round the Room' session at the Blaxall 'Ship' 1998
l to r – Rob Neal, John Howson, Reg Reeder, Katie Howson (melodeon), Jill Hill, Niki Acott

Most of the defining characteristics used to describe tradition by folk people thus contain grains of truth but none encapsulates the kernel of the matter. Tradition is not completely contained within or defined by any family, community, countryside or class. Difficulties also exist trying to analyze what is traditional by concentrating on the collected repertoire. Far too little work has been done on the sources of old English songs or the comparative antiquity of different parts of this repertoire. Too much emphasis is still being placed on questionable social history, locating field singers in home environments that those writing the commentaries (currently) can scarcely imagine over a century after the collections, with the result that too much of what the collectors recovered is now being presented as if they had invented it – songs from field singers presented as the finished article, when in reality these songs are in a state of metamorphosis – they came from somewhere and they are on a journey, in which they will surface again in a different form at some future point.

Traditionality is in short a minefield, with logical traps at every point. Is the collected song of greater of less value than one whose words or tune have been modified by a (semi) professional folksinger in modern times? Is the singer whose lettered parents came into the folk movement a generation ago and have handed their tradition on of greater or less worth than someone discovering folk music for the first time? Is a singer with a country accent of greater or less merit than a townie, even if the country singer is a new recruit to folk music and the townie has been singing for several decades? Is the recently created Border or Molly Dance worth more or less than the Cotswold dances invented by D'Arcy Ferrers at the end of C19? If it is acceptable to classify as traditional the oral singing repertoire recovered by collectors and then written down (with all the acceptance of selectivity and collector's agendas that this entails), surely written vernacular music from other sources must be equally acceptable. The conundrums are endless, so much so that it must be time to put the rule book away and conceive of English or British vernacular culture as being all of a piece, irrespective of oral or written origins.

It is thus advantageous to re-visit the approach originally put forward in Chappell's 'Popular Music of the Olden Time'. In this way, English music can be seen as a vernacular continuum stretching back into the mists before songs were first printed.

Chelmsford Morris in Cotswold kit dancing 'Upton-on-Severn stick dance' 2006

l to r – (music) Alan Wise, Keith Cilvert, (dancers) Kieran Fitzgerald, Lewis Conquer, Gordon Lunt, Simon Leach, Peter Bell, Robert Griggs, (with Thaxted M.M. behind)

Within that continuum is a series of epochs and eras in which different styles became popular for a single generation or even for many generations. A whole range of styles and subject matter can be found within the continuum, including ballads, songs, music, dances, plays, and customs. As it reflects the heritage of an entire people, the continuum has an urban as well as a rural dimension and a development line that includes creation by lettered individuals alongside transmission amongst unlettered people. Neither is the continuum entirely contained by notions of nationality – development of English vernacular culture predates both the rise of the nation state and modern centralisation. It is also not necessary to scratch very far beneath the surface to see culture (songs, dances, plays etc) travelling between locations and across national boundaries in modern times.

Prior to development of notions of 'folk' and the great early C20 collections, the continuum had creativity at its centre; arguably for a tradition to be alive creativity must be at its very core. 'Contemporary' therefore is and always has been part of 'traditional', and is necessary to ensure both preservation and development. What's more there is now no reason why new writing should not be couched in any style, past or present. In current time, it is difficult to determine what is most likely to be handed on to the upcoming generation and beyond. Even the great folk song collectors argued that the folk process involved constant selection by the people. Perhaps it is time for older notions of oral transmission to be afforded their proper

Out on Plough Monday 2003 with Good Easter Molly Gang

place in history and modern creativity accorded higher value as part of the ongoing vernacular music of England.

And the Future?

So what of the future? Well, C21 social conditions are on the move again – the pub is in decline and seemingly the club, the bedrock of folk activity for nearly a century, is under attack too, both from larger Festivals and smaller more informal gatherings. The folk song club generation is passing, both elite performers and audience / local participants, but a legacy has been left – where there was very little in 1900 or 1950, there is now ideology, a multiplicity of performance styles and a sizeable subculture which views English music in a different way from how it is presented in the mass media – particularly there are sufficient people with interest in beautiful melody, ballad style vernacular poetry, ritual plays and traditional English dance styles to ensure that these things will not pass back into the forgotten limbo from which they were rescued a century ago. Apart from anything else, a significant number of the leading performers of the current generation come from 'folk' families

Good Easter Molly Gang Music, l to r – Simon Ritchie, (? fiddle), Pete Redman, Colin Cater

Between one and two decades ago, the folk community became concerned that it was failing to hand the heritage on, and a drive to bring young performers forward began that has gathered pace subsequently. This includes competitions to unearth the most promising talent, several university first degree courses and a seemingly ever expanding adult education sector, both privately and publicly funded. Many young performers, brought up with their instruments have skills that far outweigh those of their forbears who in the main were self taught and didn't come into the music until they were in their late teens or twenties. Conversely the age at which many young performers start singing seems to be getting older. There remain enormous tasks: to re-establish linkages between folk culture and mainstream popular culture (although there are encouraging signs); also to incorporate the real history and culture of these British islands into the educational experience of young people, rather than the outdated classically oriented curriculum that sustained the country when it presided over a world Empire.

Playing a good old Suffolk one-row, keyed in C of course!

Within the folk movement , it surely is time to cast aside those things that divide and look for ways in which differing specialist interests can go forward to mutual benefit. In the last thirty years instrumental technology has made progress both electronically amplified and unamplified, so that it is reasonable to expect that performance styles will again adjust – perhaps this time changes will meet with less resistance. Stylistically the new generation of elite performers is facing outwards towards the wider community, without harming the performing opportunities of ordinary 'folkies'. Many younger folk concert performers combine exceptional musical talent with a folk musical heritage stretching back within their families. Others don't have the same family background. This doesn't matter at all. It is time to celebrate creativity, in whatever English style is available; after all we have eight hundred years of vernacular musical history, with all its richness and diversity at our disposal with which to do it. Neither should anyone complain when elite performers go off on flights of fancy in directions we might not predict in advance. On the contrary, this should be encouraged because that is how the heritage will be updated and made relevant in a contemporary setting to a mass audience. After all performer elites always existed alongside people in their communities in centuries past and continue to do so today both in this country and in Ireland and the USA. It is also true that other nations' folk music cultures are much more able to accommodate contemporary writing than is the case in England.

In the meantime, there's this old bloke called Cater, fully embedded with his community, writing songs and settings that he performs with melodeon and concertina accompaniments. The tunes and / or songs are new, though the styles are older and they have the potential to be added to the repertoire. They are a celebration of what I love best: my life with Karen and all it has brought; England's vernacular and folk heritage and customs, whatever their origins; chorus singing and dare I say it, dear old Essex with all its foibles and peculiarities. It's not for me to judge whether or not they will be taken up in the future – only to offer them into the melting pot in the hope that in time this might happen.

Thaxted Morris Men, 'all up' – 'Ring o' Bells' (Lichfield)
l to r – dancers – Roy Page, Bert Felgate, Geoff Walker, Paul Reece, Peter Donovan, Ian Anderson; music – Colin, Peter King, Dave Brewster

LIST OF REFERENCES QUOTED

1   CATER, Karen and Colin (2001 – 2009), Calendars of Traditional Customs, Hedingham Fair,
2   FRAZER, Sir J. G., (as abridged, 1922) The Golden Bough
3   MURRAY, Margaret (1917), Organisations of Witches in Great Britain, Folk Lore 28,
4   HUTTON, Ronald (1999), The Triumph of the Moon, O.U.P.
5   ROUD, Steve (2006) The English Year (Introduction p xv), Penguin
6   SHARP, Cecil (1907, new ed. Karpeles, M, 1965),
        English Folk Song: Some Conclusions, Mercury Books
7   HARKER, Dave (1985) Fakesong, Open University Press
8   SHEPARD, Leslie (1962): The Broadside Ballad, Herbert Jankins
9   HARKER, quoting KITTREDGE, George (1904), English and Scottish Popular Ballads
10   CHAPPELL, William (1859, Dover Ed, 1965), Popular Music of the Olden Time, Chappell
11   DEACON, George (1983), John Clare and the Folk Tradition, Francis Boutle
12   CHAPPELL, as above
13   THE BLIND JACK BAND (2008) Notes to CD
14   KIDSON, Frank (1891), Traditional Tunes, Chas Taphouse & Son
15   GARRETT, John M. (1976) Sixty Years of British Music Hall, Chappell
16   HOWSON, John (1992): Songs Sung in Suffolk, Veteran
17   COPPER, Bob (1995): The Copper Family Song Book – A Living Tradition, Coppersongs
18   BARCLAY, L. & JONES, I (2005): Community Dances Manual – Revised Edition, EFDSS
19   BACON, L. (1974): A Handbook of Morris Dances, The Morris Ring
20   MacCOLL, E (1990): Journeyman – an autobiography, Sidgwick & Jackson
21   LLOYD, A.L. (1952, revised 1978): Come all ye bold Miners, Lawrence & Wishart
22   EATMT (2003): Blyth Voices: Folk Songs collected in Southwold by R.Vaughan Williams
23   LLOYD, A.L. (1967): Folk Song in England, Lawrence & Wishart

OTHER SOURCES REFERRED TO

BRUCE, J. and STOKOE, J. (1882): The Northumbrian Minstrelsy
BUCHAN, Peter (1875): Ancient Ballads and Songs of the North of Scotland
CHILD, F. J. (1882 – 98, reprinted 1965) The English and Scottish Popular Ballads
DIXON, J. (1846, REPRINTED 1973): Ancient poems, ballads & songs of the Peasantry
D'URFEY, T. (1719 – 20, reprinted 1959): Wit and Mirth or Pills to Purge Melancholy
ENGEL, Carl (1866): An Introduction to the Study of National Music
HALLIWELL, J. (1851 reprinted 1973), The Yorkshire Anthology
HARLAND, J. (1865): Ballads and Songs of Lancashire
LOGAN, W. H. (1869) A Pedlar's Pack of Ballads and Songs
PERCY, Thomas (first published 1765): Reliques of Ancient English Poetry
PLAYFORD, J. (1651): The English Dancing Master
RITSON, J. (1783): A Select collection of English Songs

The Songs and Tunes

Notes

1   Penny for the Ploughboys
Written ten years ago, this song celebrates Molly Dancing, the change of the seasons and the resilience of English traditions able to adapt to changes in technology and the sometimes very harsh, uncaring attitudes of officialdom. The expression 'Penny for the Ploughboys, only once a Year, and God speed the Plough' is very old and came to me via Ashley Hutchings 'Rattlebone and Ploughjack'. When Hedingham Fair started, Karen did an illustration of Old Glory Molly Dancers using the Penny for the Ploughboys legend. The song came two or three years later. Pete Coe did me the great honour of taking it all round the country.

2   Scarborough Fair – words trad.
Happy minutes doodling in front of the stove. As with Happy and Delightful, wouldn't this song benefit from having another version? Might getting rid of the 'Parsley, Sage . . .' refrain, enable the mysteries of the riddles to be better explored?

3   Foggy Dew – words trad.
Again, a doodle by the stove. A love tune for a much loved love song.

4   High Plains of Afghanistan
Unashamedly political, written 2007, this is a remake of Lowlands of Holland to an original tune. The older I get, the more I find war utterly loathsome. If it was possible to bring down the Soviet Union and the Berlin Wall by a combination of containment and the triumph of ideas, why are troops and bullets necessary in Iraq and Afghanistan now? Britain is sending its own citizens to their deaths unnecessarily, and alienating another substantial group of its own people. I taught Muslims and others in a multicultural FE College for two decades and could palpably feel processes of radicalisation gathering pace and being fuelled by official policy. Enough!

5   Seeds of Love – words trad.
In the porch of Hambridge church, Somerset, is a plaque dedicated to the Rev. Charles Marson – the father of English folk music. Marson was the friend of Cecil Sharp and his collaborator on Folk Songs from Somerset. Seeds of Love was Sharp's first folk song collection, recovered from Marson's gardener, John England. I learned it 45 years ago from Bert Worth of Harrogate, whose guitar playing remains singular in my mind to this day. I've never quite understood why it isn't more widely sung, but it's not an easy song to master. So the idea came to make it slightly easier by constructing a new tune with a half verse chorus, rather in the manner of 'Bold Fisherman'.

6 Change at Thorpe-le-Soken

Living proof that every dark cloud has a silver lining Could anything good come out of commuting? Well actually yes, after years of standing on Shenfield station listening to the mantra "Change at Thorpe-le-Soken for Walton on the Naze", this song came one day in the 1980s in a great rush. The local folk radio programmes took it up and people remember it to this day. Originally about differences in the pace of life (with some apologies to W. H. Davies 'We have no time to stand and stare'), I now feel that being 'on the Naze' is a state of mind you can experience anywhere – anything that keeps you away from progress, particularly of the built up kind. I often tailor the words to the place in which I'm singing the song. The tune owes something to the East Anglian song 'Fella that plays the Trombone'.

7 Benbow's March

Originally conceived as part of a song accompaniment to the 'Sailed to Virginia' song version of Benbow's death, this tune somehow grew a second part in 2008

8 Tricky Dicky Polka

Written in the 1970s to celebrate one of my heroes – well at least Nixon was a transparent crook who got caught more than once, unlike many politicians since. These two tunes have been used by several ceilidh bands over the years.

&

9 Liberation Polka

I must have had Mike Oldfield in mind writing this. I wish I could do it again now!

10 Number Two Top Seam – words: Roger Watson.

Part of Roger's garland of Nottinghamshire Songs, written in mid 1960s from stories and urban myths then circulating in north Notts. A chilling tale that was everybody's worst fear, originally set to 'Tramps and Hawkers'. This tune written in the mid 1960s.

11 Derby Footrace – words trad.

When I lived in Clay Cross, Derbyshire (1967-70), I became friendly with Frank Sutton of Dronfield, at that time a walking reliquary of information on all things folk connected with Derbyshire or South Yorkshire. Frank had a great passion for the work of Llewellyn Jewitt, the C19 Derbyshire luminary, founder of the Derby Telegraph and author of Ballads and Songs of Derbyshire (1867), from which the words of the song come. A typical broadside it is described as "A new song on the great Foot Race that was contested on the London Road, near Derby, on the 18th day of March 1822, betwixt Jas. Wantling of Derby, and Shaw, the Staffordshire Hero for two hundred Guineas" . Roger and I sang it occasionally in the 1960s to a pretty ordinary tune, with this offering only happening by chance decades later, because Keith Kendrick was coming to guest at Essex Singers Club. Keith took it home and, bless him, has been singing it ever since.

12 Wassail

A morning's relaxation at Whitby Festival in 2005, this song was inspired partly by Jim Causley's Whimple Wassail song, but also grew out of an increasing awareness that travelling groups of Wassailers might include any skills that the participants might have – singing, step dancing etc. Linking Mumming plays with sword dancing still survives in some places, but there is every reason to suppose that people once went out Wassailing all over England and (the English speaking parts of) Wales, and that now it's coming back. Like other winter songs I've put together it celebrates the turn of the year, rather than being from the perspective of any single religion.

13   Lizzie Wan – words trad.

How can anyone look through the wonderful Child Ballads without wanting to stitch verses together and make their own ballad versions up? As well as the new tune, I was intrigued to find linking verses that describe Lizzie's murder, as well as the superb 'sun and the moon' ending.

14   Happy and Delightful – words trad.

I first learned Pleasant and Delightful from Louis Killen's peerless rendition on 'Hootenany in London', since when it has become a standard with almost no other version circulating. This seems slightly strange to me, as in times gone by variants of many songs spread like seeds in the wind developed by chapmen and country singers alike. When one afternoon I sat down doodling, concertina in hand, and a new tune / arangement emerged, nothimg could have seemed more natural. Why not two versions?

15   The Merry Actors

A song to celebrate the Mummers' art. In 2005 Karen developed a still life image, featuring many of the joys of Christmas – top hat and feathers, wine, ivy and mince pies. We decided to call it Mince Pies Hot, Mince Pies Cold, and as with one or two other images it provided the inspiration for a song, unusually with two choruses. The song follows the plot of many Mummers plays through, with the customary cadge in return for good luck at the end – well almost, you might hear the final chorus anywhere the Mummers go, though it's not guaranteed.

16   Glastonbury – tune trad.

The only song written from an overtly Christian perspective, albeit an apocryphal one The Legend of Joseph of Arimathea and Jesus visiting Glastonbury, bringing with them the Holy Thorn, which blooms on Christmas Day, is well known. It is celebrated in Glastonbury every year. Karen produced an image in 2003 and we both thought it would be a good idea to tie it to the 'I saw three ships' carol – after all the Somerset levels were once flooded and Glastonbury would have been accessible from the Bristol Channel. Another chance to wish all wars away.

17   May Song

Recently written (2008 – 9) and based on ideas in many other traditional May Songs, this offering does its best to eliminate God – he gets a good airing in other places – to celebrate as many May customs as possible and to offer a whole year blessing by following the year round. We visualise this song as a processional, disappearing into the hole in the middle of the record like all the best old Elvis numbers

18   Jenny Wren

An overtly Pagan song. In 1986, Norman Isles wrote the book 'Who really killed Cock Robin?' He put forward the idea that Christianity had no customs of its own and that a large part of the church calendar and songs, together with most nursery rhymes had been blagged from earlier Pagan tradition. Wouldn't it be a good idea to rewrite the songs and blag them back? As part of his thesis he developed the idea of Jenny Wren as the spirit of the people and the earth and suggested the 'Seven Joys of Mary' as a possible candidate for being rewritten. I didn't need any more prompting.

19   Steam with Santa

Santa Claus, my hero, I don't think. The spirit of Christmas grasping! I've wanted to write a song called "When Santa gets his claws into you" for years but it wouldn't ever come. My vision of the red coated pest, leering over young children and stinking of beer and fags won't go away, it's probably a subconscious childhood memory. A couple of miles up the road, the Colne Valley Railway, a splendid railway preservation society with about a mile of track hold an annual bash called 'Steam with Santa' for about four weekends just before Christmas. We drive past the sign every year, and I'd thought "there's a song in there somewhere" for some time. Eventually my imagination got the better of me.

PENNY FOR THE PLOUGHBOYS

Chorus

On St Stephens Day (Boxing Day), after dark, **Old Glory Molly Dancers** form a silent torchlit procession to the sound of a single drum to The Bell PH, Middleton, nr Yoxford Suffolk, to perform the 'Cutty Wren'. A large crowd has gathered for the Molly dancing, singing and story telling, and to see the 'Wren House'. The ceremony symbolizes the turn of the year, before work starts again. after Christmas. Old Glory were the first Molly dancers to take up 'Penny for the Ploughboys' as their anthem

1. PENNY FOR THE PLOUGHBOYS

Words & tune by Colin Cater

At the turn of the year all the fields were brown in the days when I was young
With corn in the barns, frost in the ground and never a green shoot sprung
Then the ploughmen came with their hobnailed boots and the Molly dance rich and slow
And with magical plays and songs of the land they bade the corn to grow

Chorus
Only once a year, penny for the ploughboys
To keep us in good cheer and multiply the grain
Only once a year, penny for the ploughboys
Speed the plough till the year turns round again

Then they ploughed, they sowed, they harrowed him in 'till the rain from heaven did fall
The wind did blow, and the sun did shine and he soon grew amazing tall
When the corn was ripened the harvesters came and the barns and the breweries rang
And when all was safely gathered in they raised their voice and sang.
Chorus

Now the seasons are all changed round, a slave to the great machines
The fields are ploughed in the high summer time, by the turn of the year they're green
Gone are the trades, the horses and families that followed the seasons along
And the old pubs close 'cos they can't resound to the fiddle or a country song.
Chorus

But there's strength in the plays, the dances and songs that have lasted a thousand years.
There's strength in barley, malt and hops brewed into a country beer.
It puts a spring in the step of an old Straw Bear, makes the dancer leap for the skies
And when the Molly Gangs come to speed the plough, they raise their glass and cry.
Chorus

2. SCARBOROUGH FAIR

Words Traditional, tune & arrangement by Colin Cater

Are you going to Scarborough Fair, remember me to one who lives there
Remember me to one who lives there, for once she was a true lover of mine

Tell her to make me a cambric shirt, without any seam or needlework
Without any seam or needlework and then she'll be a true lover of mine

Tell her to wash it in a dry well, where water ne'er sprung nor drop of rain fell
Where water ne'er sprung nor drop of rain fell and then she'll be a true lover of mine

Tell her to dry it on a sharp thorn which never bore blossom since Adam was born
Which ne'er bore blossom since Adam was born and then she'll be a true lover of mine

Are you going to Scarborough Fair, remember me to one who lives there
Remember me to one who lives there, for once she was a true lover of mine

Will you buy me an acre of land between the salt water and the sea strand
Between the salt water and the sea strand or you'll never be a true lover of mine

And will you plough it with a lamb's horn and sow it all over with one peppercorn
And sow it all over with one peppercorn or you'll never be a true lover of mine

And will you reap it with a sickle of leather and tie it all up with a peacock's feather
And tie it all up with a peacock's feather or you'll never be a true lover of mine

And when you've done and finished your work, you can come to me for your cambric shirt
You can come to me for your cambric shirt, for then you'll be a true lover of mine

Are you going to Scarborough Fair, remember me to one who lives there
Remember me to one who lives there, for once she was a true lover of mine

3. FOGGY DEW

Words Traditional, tune & arrangement by Colin Cater

When I was a bachelor, airy and young, I followed the roving trade
The only harm I ever done was to court a fair young maid
I wooed her all the summer season and part of the winter too
And the only harm I ever done was to keep her from the foggy dew

One night as I lay on my bed, taking my balmy sleep
This pretty fair maid came to my bedhead and bitterly she did weep
She wept, she mourned, she tore her hair, she cried "What shall I do?"
So all that night I kept her there, just to keep her from the foggy dew

And in the first part of the night we did sport and play
Then in the second part of the night, snug in my arms she lay
And when broad daylight did appear she cried "I am undone"
"Hold your tongue you silly young girl, for the foggy dew is gone

"Supposing you was to have a child it would make you laugh and smile
Supposing you was to have another, it would make you think a while
Supposing you was to have another, another and another one too
It would make you leave off these foolish young tricks and think on the foggy dew"

Now I loved that girl with all my heart, as dear as my lovely life
But in the second part of the year, she became another man's wife
I never told him of her faults, and I never intend to do
But many's the time when she winks at me and smiles, I remember the foggy dew

4. HIGH PLAINS OF AFGHANISTAN

Words & tune by Colin Cater

On the night I was married as I lay on my bed
An advert came on the screen, these words to me it said
"Arise, arise young married man and come along with me
To the high plains of Afghanistan to fight your enemy"

But the high plains are a barren place with the mountains ringed around with snow
You might be scorched in the midday sun, but at night it falls degrees below
And the soldiers are a bonny bunch, full of merry laughter as they go
To the high plains of Afghanistan to fight the daring foe

They called air strikes on the Taliban to drive them away
But the snipers' bullets and the rocket powered grenades still rain down every day
And my love was killed by a roadside bomb that blew his armoured car away
He's home now, laid beneath the Union Flag while the slow march does play

I have friends who came from Pakistan; they go to the Mosque to pray
They see soldiers in British uniforms fighting Muslims every day
And the young men are getting angrier, cos it's always in the news
They love this country and the God they serve, and they can't see why they have to choose

There's no therapist or chocolatier or fine conditioner for my hair
No designer labels or holidays abroad can ease my heart's despair
Nor neither will I marry again until the day I die
Since the high plains of Afghanistan have parted my love and I

5. SEEDS OF LOVE

Words Traditional, tune & arrangement by Colin Cater

I sowed the seeds of love and I sowed them in the spring
In April, May and June likewise, the small birds they do sing
The small birds they do sing, the small birds they do sing
In April, May and June likewise, the small birds they do sing

My garden is planted well with flowers everywhere
But I had not the right to choose for myself of the ones that I loved dear
Of the ones that I loved dear, of the ones that I loved dear
But I had not the right to choose for myself of the ones that I loved dear

My gardener was standing by and I bade him choose for me
He chose me the violet the lily and the pink but these I refused all three
But these I refused all three, but these I refused all three
He chose me the violet the lily and the pink but these I refused all three

For in June there's the red rosebud and that's the flower for me
So I picked and I plucked at the red and rosey bush till I gained the willow tree
Till I gained the willow tree, till I gained the willow tree
So I picked and I plucked at the red and rosey bush till I gained the willow tree

For the willow it will twist and the willow it will twine
And I wish I was in the young man's arms that has this heart of mine
That has this heart of mine, that has this heart of mine
And I wish I was in the young man's arms that has this heart of mine

Then I locked up my garden gate and resolved to keep the key
Till another young man came courting me and he stole my heart away
He stole my heart away, he stole my heart away
Till another young man came courting me and he stole my heart away

Now my garden is overrun, no flowers in it grew
For the beds that once were covered in thyme, are now overrun with rue
They are now overrun with rue, they are now overrun with rue
For the beds that once were covered in thyme, are now overrun with rue

So come all you false young men don't leave me here to complain
For the grass that once was trodden underfoot, give it time it will rise again
Give it time it will rise again, give it time it will rise again
For the grass that once was trodden underfoot, give it time it will rise again

6. CHANGE AT THORPE LE SOKEN

Words & tune by Colin Cater

I've been a countryman all my life, Essex is where I dwell
Whenever I go to London town, it's worse than being in Hell
For I get crushed to death on the Underground and I always lose my way
And I long to get back to Liverpool Street to hear the announcer say

Chorus
You've got to change at Thorpe-Le-Soken for Walton on the Naze
Sometimes when the train breaks down you can wait a couple of days
But you won't ever suffer jet lag with your body all out of phase
If you change at Thorpe-Le-Soken for Walton on the Naze

Now I don't know why folk rush about with their hearts so full of care
Me I stand by the railway line and I always have time to stare
To say 'Good-day' to the morning briefcases and pretty girls so sweet
Watch the fields of shimmering green turn to billowing seas of wheat

Chorus

London's greatly altered now, expanding every day
Toytown houses cover the fields and the villages wither away
It's hard to find a country pub where you think you can belong
For a pint and a chat and a game of crib, and sometimes a bit of a song

Chorus

7. BENBOW'S MARCH

By Colin Cater

Session at the
'John O' Gaunt',
Sutton, Beds
Mary Humphreys
(English concertina),
Colin, Anahata
(behind with drinks)

8. TRICKY DICKY
By Colin Cater

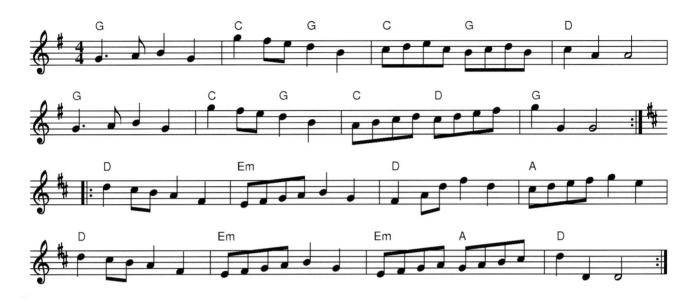

9. LIBERATION POLKA
By Colin Cater

10. NUMBER TWO TOP SEAM

words by Roger Watson, tune by Colin Cater

As I was out a-walking, one evening in the Spring
I overheard a collier, most mournfully did sing
I stopped and listened for a while to what he had to say
And I never will forget his words until my dying day

I was born here in this town, I've lived here all my life
I had three fine young children likewise a loving wife
My father was a collier and so I followed him down
And I worked the Number Two Top Seam right underneath the town

All the houses in our street they had cracks in every wall
And people always used to say, some day they all might fall
For sometimes in the dead of night disturbing every dream
You colud hear the blast from every shot in the Number Two Top Seam

It was as the shift was changing, at half past four one day
The roof collapsed behind them when a timber prop gave way
But it wasn't till we reached the top that the dreadful truth we found
That half a street fell fifteen feet and landed beneath the ground

There were children playing in that street, there were women in their homes
When the roof collapsed beneath them in a hail of bricks and stones
There was nothing left but ruins where our houses once had been
And twenty women and children lay in the Number Two Top Seam

Well they say they'll give us all new homes at what they call great cost
But that is little recompense for the loved ones we have lost
Young colliers who've a mind to wed, consider ere you do
That the pits not only claim the men but the women and the children too

11. DERBY FOOTRACE

Broadside printed in 'Derbyshire Ballads' by Llewellynn Jewitt 1867, tune by Colin Cater

Well the eighteenth day of March my lads will long be handed down
When thousands came from miles around into famed Derby town
To see the Great Footrace be run for a hundred guineas a side
Twixt Shaw the Stafford hero and Wantling, Derby's pride

Chorus
Fol-de-rol, fol-de-ray, to Derby make your way
To see the two great heroes run the Great Footrace today

And now the day it is drew nigh when the heroes try their skill
When thousands flock around the streets, wagering who will
Great sums they are laid down my boys, ere they begin to run
In mingled shouts you'll hear them cry "I take your bet" and "Done!"
Chorus

And now we see them striving, which one will get there first
Straining vein and muscle till their lungs must almost burst
Wantling takes the lead and he labours hard to gain
The money for his friends and to establish his own fame
Chorus

And now the race is over and the women, men and boys
Cry "Wantling now for ever" in shouts that rend the skies
His name today is lifted up as a runner of great fame
For Shaw the Stafford hero had been beat by him again
Chorus

You noble lads of Staffordshire who backed Shaw in that day
And ventured all your money, leaving none of your shots to pay
Be wiser for the future if again you chance to come
And bring more money with you lads, lest you go empty home
Chorus

WASSAIL

Chorus

12. WASSAIL

Words & tune by Colin Cater

We've been travelling this country by the light of the moon
And we hope you are ready, that we haven't come too soon
We've brought fiddlers and dancers and a great many more
Please let us come in for it's cold at your door

Chorus
It's your wassail, our wassail
Joy come to you and a jolly wassail
Come fill up our bowls now with cider and beer
And we wish you many blessings till we come again next year

The Quack Doctor is here with a top hat on his head
Prince Paradine will fight again though he was dead
With King George, Lord Nelson, the Wild Horse and Old Tosspot
And Old Father Christmas who will never be forgot

Chorus

When our play it is over we will end with a song
And dance with our rapiers that are hard, sharp and long
When the swords are raised high all the company will cheer
It's a mark of our unity over hundreds of years

Chorus

For the year it is turning and the new Sun is born
To return soon to ripen our apples and corn
With beer bread and cider, we'll bless orchard and field
That a plentiful harvest in time they will yield

Chorus

We wish health and prosperity and long life to give
To this great house and everyone that in it does live
And to all this fine company that dwell far and near
Bright Yule, Merry Christmas and a Happy New Year

Chorus

13. LIZZIE WAN

Words Traditional, tune & arrangement by Colin Cater

Fair Lizzie she sits in her own bower door weeping and making moan
And by there came her brother dear, "what ails thee, Lizzie Wan?"

"I ail and I ail, brother dear, I ail, I'll tell you the reason why
For there is a babe between my sides that's of you dear Billy and I"

"What have you told my father? what have you told my mother? What did you tell on me?"
Then he's lifted up his great broad sword that hung down by his knee
And he's cutted off fair Lizzie Wan's head and her body he's made in three

"Where have you been and what have you done, my son my Geordie Wan?
For I see by your colour and the light that's in your eye, some fell deed you have done

What's that blood on the point of your sword, my son come tell to me?"
"That is the blood of my greyhound; he would not run for me"

"But your greyhound's blood was never so red, my son come tell to me?"
"That is the blood of my grey mare; no more will she hunt with me"

"But your grey mare's blood was never so fresh, my son come tell to me?"
"It is not the blood of my horse or my hound; it's the blood of our Lizzie"

"What will you do when your father comes to know, my son come tell to me?"
"I will set my foot on the tallest ship and sail far beyond the sea"

"When will you to your own home return, my son come tell to me?"
"When the sun and the moon dance down upon the green and I pray that will never be"

14. HAPPY AND DELIGHTFUL

Words Traditional, tune & arrangement by Colin Cater

It was happy and delightful on a midsummer's morn
When the green fields and the meadows they were burdened with corn
And the blackbirds and thrushes sang on every green spray
And the larks sang most melodious at the dawning of the day
And the larks sang most melodious at the dawning of the day

A sailor and his true love were out walking one fine day
Said the sailor to his true love "I am bound far away
I am bound for the Indies where the cannons loudly do roar
I must go now and leave you Nancy, you're the girl that I adore
I must go now and leave you Nancy, you're the girl that I adore"

Then a ring from off'n' her finger she immediately drew
Saying "take this dearie William and my heart will go too"
And as he embraced her tears from her eyes fell
Saying "May I go along with you", "O no my love farewell"
Saying "May I go along with you", "O no my love farewell"

Then it's "Fare thee well lovely Nancy for I can no longer stay
For the topsails they are hoisted and the anchor's aweigh
And the big ship lays waiting for the next flowing tide
And if even I return love I will make you my bride
And if even I return love I will make you my bride"

THE MERRY ACTORS

78

Chorus 1

Chorus 2

15. THE MERRY ACTORS

Words & tune by Colin Cater

Chorus 1
Mince Pies Hot, mince pies cold
Mince pies in the oven and they're nine days old
Who needs mince pies, none can tell,
But Little Jolly Jack and Me

Chorus 2
For we are the Merry Actors and we come with courage bold
And we're here to entertain you, like we've been since the days of old

In comes I Old Father Christmas with my long white beard and sack
They've often tried to banish me but I always will come back
And I'll bring you a present for the ones you love and plenty of good cheer
For I'm here to welcome the new-born Sun and the turning of the year
Chorus 1 & 2

In Comes I St George the Champion and I come from the Mediterraen
I'm George for Georgia, George for Greece, for Portugal and Spain
But I nailed my colours to an English mast at Crecy and Agincourt
And I'll fight for the right of everybody here, whether they be rich or poor
Chorus 1

In comes I, the Black Prince of Paradise, of honour and renown
I'm here to challenge Bold St George and to wear the Champion's crown
And I bring you the promise of a brave new world, my sword is tempered steel
And I'll fight for the right of the world to change like an ever turning wheel
Chorus 1 & 2

It's time for the Old Quack Doctor, with his bottle of elecampane
For George and the Black Prince both are dead and soon must rise again
One kiss from the Doctor will bring them back, but all their wars must cease
For the time of the Champions is all worn out and the world must live in peace
Chorus 1

Now here's Beelzebub with his dripping pan and club, he'll scare your kids away
And Little Jolly Jack with his family on his back will call another day
So put your hands in your pockets, and dig us out a quid, for we wants a drop of good beer
And we'll wish you good luck for the next twelve months, till we call again next year
Chorus 1 & 2

For we are the geriatrics, with our Zimmer Frames so bold
And we're here to entertain you, even though we are all incredibly old

GLASTONBURY

16. GLASTONBURY

Words by Colin Cater, tune Traditional.

As I sat on a sunny bank,
On Christmas Day, On Christmas Day
As I sat on a sunny bank,
On Christmas Day in the morning

I saw three ships come sailing in,
On Christmas Day, On Christmas Day
I saw three ships come sailing in,
On Christmas Day in the morning

And who was in those ships all three
On Christmas Day, On Christmas Day
But Jesus and Joseph of Arimathee
On Christmas Day in the morning

And they sailed into Glastonbury
On Christmas Day, On Christmas Day
And they sailed into Glastonbury
On Christmas Day in the morning

They brought a staff of Lebanese Thorn
On Christmas Day, On Christmas Day
They brought a staff of Lebanese Thorn
On Christmas Day in the morning

They planted it on Wearyall Hill
On Christmas Day, On Christmas Day
And to this day it grows there still
On Christmas Day in the morning

And every year it blossoms and blooms
On Christmas Day, On Christmas Day
And every year it blossoms and blooms
On Christmas Day in the morning

That wars all over the world might cease
On Christmas Day, On Christmas Day
And everybody can live in peace
On Christmas Day in the morning

82

17. MAY SONG

Words & tune by Colin Cater

We have been out in the woods all night and part of the long summers' day
And now we're returning home again, we've brought you a bunch of May

Our bunch of May is a garland gay, and before your door it stands
It's nothing but a sprout, but it's well budded out by the Lord of the Greenwood's hands

Some will lift their banners up and raise them to the sky
Some will caper up the Sun, then drink old England dry

For today it is the first of May, it's time for a holiday
With a fine parade and a great big fair we'll crown our Queen of the May

When the fields are turned to yellow and brown and Barleycorn is slain
From the nut brown bowl we'll drink his blood, send it back to the land again

When the days grow short, the stars are bright and a fine yellow Moon shines down
Fruits from the harvest will keep us warm until the year turns round

In the ice cold times when the snow flies fast and the Northern winds do blow
You can hear the sound of the new born lambs; see the primrose through the snow

Now the year it is almost round, and we can no longer stay
We'll bless you all both great and small, and wish you a joyful May

May-day customs –
clockwise from top right:
Awaking the Jack, with the
Motley Morris, Bluebell
Hill, Rochester, Kent; May
blossom; Trade Unions
Marches; Hastings Jack-in-
the-Green; May Garland;
May-pole dancing (centre);
Chimney Sweeps proces-
sion; May Queens; Padstow
hobby horse, Cornwall;
Minehead hobby horse,
Somerset

18. JENNY WREN

Words & tune by Colin Cater

Chorus

The first great joy that Jenny Wren brought was the joy of one
With Holly and Ivy that grow in the wood, Yuletide had begun
Yuletide had begun and merry shall we be
With Holly and Ivy that grow in the wood for all the world to see

The next great joy that Jenny Wren brought was the joy of two
Food to eat and fuel to burn to last the winter through
To last all the winter and merry shall we be
With Holly and Ivy that grow in the wood for all the world to see

The next great joy that Jenny Wren brought was the joy of three
Wine and cider and lashings of beer and we'll go on a spree
And we'll get plastered and merry shall we be
With Holly and Ivy that grow in the wood for all the world to see

The next great joy that Jenny Wren brought was the joy of four
To journey with the giver of gifts and bless the children all
Bless all the children and merry shall they be
With Holly and Ivy that grow in the wood for all the world to see

The next great joy that Jenny Wren brought was the joy of five
Magicians and singers and tellers of tales to keep the old ways alive
To keep them alive and merry shall we be
With Holly and Ivy that grow in the wood for all the world to see

The next great joy that Jenny Wren brought was the joy of six
King George is dead and risen again by an old Quack Doctor's tricks
He's always full of tricks and merry shall he be
With Holly and Ivy that grow in the wood for all the world to see

The last great joy that Jenny Wren brought was the joy of seven
Moon and stars up in the sky till the Sun returns again
And the year turns round and merry shall we be
With Holly and Ivy that grow in the wood for all the world to see

STEAM WITH SANTA

Chorus

19. STEAM WITH SANTA

Words & tune by Colin Cater

There is a little railway in the north of Essex county
It's only got a mile of track but they have a winter bounty
There's lots of mulled wine and mince pies and everyone is jolly
Because they deck the carriages with mistletoe and holly

And you can . . .
Steam with Santa, every weekend from November
Steam with Santa, it's a day out to remember
Steam with Santa, hear that lonesome whistle blow
Christmas comes round yearly, lasts for a couple of months or so

It used to run from Haverhill along the river Colne
Sometimes you'd travel with a couple of sheep, sometimes you'd be alone
Then came Doctor Beeching with his great big hairy axe
And closed all the rural railways and they grubbed up all the tracks

But you can . . .
Steam with Santa, you'll get lots of presents
Look out of the window see the rabbits, rats and pheasants
Steam with Santa, it's a moment of elation
Like being on the Flying Scotsman when you're stood outside a station

Now Santa has to operate by the modern credo
There's lots of police checks on him to make sure he's not a paedo
And Santa's reindeer think his carbon fotprint isn't cool
Now they can't have their nightly fix of aviation fu-u-el

But you can . . .
Steam with Santa, come and join his fan club
And if you're good he'll let you have a rummage in his bran tub
You might get an MP4, but shouldn't ever quibble
If the present you unwrap came from a boot fair down in Sible

And finally when Christmas comes and all the world is stuffing
Santa's sack is empty and his reindeer have got nuffin'
And while you're snoring at the Queen, he's packing up his traps and
Then he'll drive to Stansted and fly business class to Lapland

But you can . . .
Steam with Santa, thank the world for Coca Cola
MacDonalds, Sony, Virgin, Vodafone and Motorola
Steam with Santa, hear that lonesome whistle blow
Christmas comes round yearly, lasts for a couple of months or so

The Recordings

Live Recording:
The Three Horseshoes, Duton Hill, Essex on March 25th 2009

Colin Cater; Vocals, Melodeons, and Anglo Concertina
Karen Cater; Vocals, Percussion

The Chorus:
Niki & Mike Acott; Julie & Mike; Elaine Barker; Dave Bartlett & Linda Baddeley; Stan Bloor; Cathy & Keith Carpenter; Robin & Gill Carpenter; Keith Cilvert; John Clark; Sue & Ray Clark; Dave Cooper; Sue & John Cubbin; Terry & Linda Dix; Mary & Gordon; Libby Byne-Grey; John Grey; Pete & Annie Harding; Alan Hardy; Lynne Heraud; Adrian Hilton; Joe Hobbs; Mary Humphreys & Anahata; Ken Hunnybun; Brian & Christine Kell; Richard Legge; Paul McCann; Adrian May; Maggie Moore; Paul O'Kelly; Roy Page; Dave & Jan Ponting; Ruth Price; Paul & Marion Reece; Simon & Bobby Ritchie; Kiti & Derek Theobald; Peter & Hazel Waghorn; Geoff & Maureen Walker; Mike Wilkinson

Studio recording:

Treewind Studios, Fordham, Cambridgeshires on 5th April 2009 and 28th April 2009.

The Musicians:
Colin Cater; Vocals, Melodeons, and Anglo Concertina
Karen Cater; Vocals, Percussion and banjo
Anahata; Cello and Melodeon
Mary Humphreys; English Concertina and banjo
Dave Holland; Fiddle

All recordings engineered and mixed by Anahata – *and a wonderful job he did too!*

"I bought my first Hohner, a 'pokerwork', in the 1970s in a shop on the Leytonstone High Road during a college lecturers strike. I still play it. Forty years is a long time to have a pokerwork, in fact."

Colin's Instruments

"All my melodeons are old Hohners, most of them are older than me. I like the sound they make – sort of flatulent!"

"Older than you and more flatulent!" – Karen

a. Hohner A/D (the latest addition)
b. Anglo concertina in C/G by Colin Dipper 1974
c. Hohner G/D red pearloid
d. Anglo concertina G/D By Morse (USA) 2006

e. Hohner Pokerwork G/D 1975 (the original)
f. Anglo concertina Bb/F by Jeffries
g. Hohner Erika C/F
h. Hohner Club Eb/Bb-ish (the "Steam Organ")
All other Hohners built between 1930 and 1950-ish

Live Recording –
the Three Horseshoes,
Duton Hill,
25th March 2009

Treewind Studio,
Fordham,
Cambs
5th April 2009
28th April 2009

"Look at the bells
on that!"

Acknowledgements

Photographs

Many of the photographs used in this book have been in Colin's possession for more years than he would care to own up to. Consequently he has no idea who took some of them, or where they came from. If you are reading this and recognise a particular photo as being one you took, we apologise most profusely at having quite unintentionally failed to credit you and beg your forgiveness – no offence was intended.

Identifiable photos by:
Karen Cater, BBC, Cath Ingham, Jim Etheridge, Dave Russell, Ann Ward, Tim Hatcher, Marion Reece, Sheffield Star, Sarah Graves, Chris Mewse, Aly Mewse

Artwork

Most of the artwork is © Karen Cater for Hedingham Fair
Poster design p25 – Sarah Graves
other pictures from Broadside ballad sheets

Index

Penny for the Ploughboys

The CD tracks

1. **Wassail :**
   Colin, vocal & C/F melodeon; Karen, tambourine; Chorus
2. **Scarborough Fair :**
   Colin, vocal & A/D melodeon; Karen, vocal
3. **Seeds of Love :**
   Colin, vocal & C/F melodeon; Karen, vocal; Chorus
4. **Penny for the Ploughboys :**
   Colin, vocal & C/F melodeon; Chorus
5. **High Plains of Afghanistan :**
   Colin, vocal & C/F melodeon
6. **Tricky Dicky Polka / Liberation Polka :**
   Colin, D/G melodeon; Karen, spoons; Mary, English Concertina; Anahata, D/G melodeon & cello; Dave, fiddle
7. **Happy and Delightful :**
   Colin, vocal & Anglo Concertina; Chorus
8. **May Song :**
   Colin, vocal & C/F melodeon; Karen, bodhran & Morris bells; Mary, banjo; Anahata, cello; Dave, fiddle
9. **Foggy Dew :**
   Colin, vocal & C/F melodeon; Karen, banjo; Mary, English Concertina; Anahata, cello; Dave, fiddle
10. **Benbow's March :**
    Colin, C/F melodeon; Karen, tambourine; Mary, English Concertina; Anahata, cello; Dave, fiddle
11. **Jenny Wren :**
    Colin, vocal & C/F melodeon; Karen, tambourine; Chorus
12. **Glastonbury :**
    Colin, vocal & C/F melodeon; Chorus
13. **The Merry Actors :**
    Colin, vocal & C/F melodeon; Chorus
14. **Steam with Santa :**
    Colin, vocal & C/F melodeon; Karen, train whistle
15. **Change at Thorpe-le-Soken :**
    Colin, vocal & C/F melodeon; Chorus

bonus track – Penny for the Ploughboys *(by popular demand)*
   Colin, vocal & Bb / Eb melodeon; Karen, vocal; Chorus